# REPLICATION

## THE ART and SCIENCE of FRANCHISING YOUR BUSINESS

# HAROLD B MILLER

# REPLICATION
## THE ART AND SCIENCE OF FRANCHISING YOUR BUSINESS

iUniverse books may be ordered through booksellers or by contacting:

iUniverse
1663 Liberty Drive
Bloomington, IN 47403
www.iuniverse.com
844-349-9409

Because of the dynamic nature of the Internet, any web addresses or links contained in this book may have changed since publication and may no longer be valid. The views expressed in this work are solely those of the author and do not necessarily reflect the views of the publisher, and the publisher hereby disclaims any responsibility for them.

Any people depicted in stock imagery provided by Getty Images are models, and such images are being used for illustrative purposes only.
Certain stock imagery © Getty Images.

ISBN: 978-1-6632-3738-5 (sc)
ISBN: 978-1-6632-3737-8 (e)

Library of Congress Control Number: 2022905229

Print information available on the last page.

iUniverse rev. date: 03/21/2022

# CONTENTS

# CHAPTER 1

# IS YOUR BUSINESS MODEL REPLICABLE?

Being an entrepreneur and system builder, you spend endless hours honing and perfecting your business model and methods. When you have achieved greatness with a profitable business model and have accomplished the hardest parts—including sales execution, profitability, talent acquisition, internal and external systems, and operations performance—and are thinking of ways to scale, a big question arises: "Should I clone this?"

I am a franchise consultant and strategic planner. Nothing is more disappointing for me than to see motivated and brilliant entrepreneurs get taken advantage of by individuals or companies who encourage them to scale when they are clearly not ready, whether because a scalable version of their business is not properly designed and defined, or because they do not have the dedicated capital to expand.

Having strong consulting and legal representation prior to launching a franchise is crucial to your success. Such representation not only helps you to avoid the mistakes that would be obvious to any seasoned franchise professional. It also can bring to light larger issues you have not thought of yet. There are many details to be explored before you ask another entity to buy or operate a duplicate model of your creation.

I have written this book as a franchise industry consultant and CEO. My business is to take franchise-able businesses that wish to build themselves into a multi-unit success and bring them to market. I assist them to consider strategic planning, legal, operations, training, market studies, marketing plans, sales training, management training, and many other customized functions required for the industry-specific needs of their model.

Because of my experience with the wide variety of challenges that are uncovered in every franchise development, it was suggested to me that I distill this experience into a book that may benefit entrepreneurs who are carefully weighing their options for the fulfillment of their dreams.

Is your business worth replicating? Is it in demand to the point where it needs to be all over your state, your country, or the world? Does a concept need to be unique to be successful? Or, as I recently screamed at a training seminar, do we really need yet another yogurt variation?

I currently represent clients in fields as diverse as pizza, weight loss, K–12 education, medicine, refinishing services, and coffee. I can say with full confidence that a franchise does not need to be unique to be viable for scaling. What it does need is a solid product or service and key differentiators that make it competitive in the larger market. It does not need to be the first of its kind. Even pizza places and hamburger joints have a lot of room for properly targeted growth by means of interesting twists on the most mature of franchise models.

Let's do a little homework together before we dive into how to develop a franchise. With modern tools, it is inexcusable for even the most daring business builder to launch without doing at least one respectable analysis of their market. In many cases, a complete market study is crucial. Some very smart entrepreneurs spike a market by first planting an additional test location in an area from which they can gather the best data. They may even build three or four locations when capital is available. This is a fantastic approach if you can afford it and have the time to wait.

The fact is your market does not wait for you. If you are scaling into a demand marketplace, building additional locations by yourself can be the kiss of death. Consider cautiously developing each market through franchising. Each situation is different, and some concepts really do need live unit testing as a part of their market research. Later in this book, I will talk about key methods of studying your franchise market, the importance of gathering and assimilating your own data, and how to think about demographic and psychographic studies.

But for the moment, let's talk about *you*!

## Why Do You Want to Franchise Your Model?

There are potentially dozens of business reasons to franchise a concept. I am going to focus on five key motivators that drive the franchisors of today.

### Capital

At the end of the day, start-up capital is the number-one reason to scale your business through franchising. A corporate model is another way to go, but this will involve obtaining capital in the form of loans, outside investment that erodes your ownership percentage, or tapping family and friends with deep pockets.

Franchise development will cost a substantial amount for building the business structure and operation. But once these are set up and running, franchisees will invest their capital for the privilege of being awarded a franchise or multiple franchises within your system. Trading full corporate ownership of a small number of units for the rewards of franchise royalties derived from a sizable chain of stores is one of the most popular business models in the world. It works brilliantly in hundreds of business categories.

### Rapid Growth

Once you focus on franchise sales, franchisee training, and franchise support, the growth model is in constant motion. Franchise fees obtained at the beginning of each sale propel the payment of costs, while ongoing royalties support the operation once scaled to profitability. There is no business or distribution system that scales faster than franchising.

*Talent*

When you hire employees for a corporate model, they can leave at any time. The entire management responsibility is firmly on your shoulders, even if you have tremendously competent managers running your system for you. Franchisees represent a different level of motivated talent. They have tapped their 401(k), taken a home loan, or in some other way raised funds to buy into your business system and brand. With proper franchisee selection and training, this is a recipe for a highly motivated work force with full management responsibility and accountability.

Some companies that have more than enough revenue to scale without franchising do it anyway, just to gain the motivated talent pool. For a new developer wishing to teach a highly motivated, long-term workforce, franchising is even more appetizing.

*Exit Strategy*

Many entrepreneurs have spent their best and happiest days building their systems of business. They want to hand the keys to the store to motivated managers who will build the franchise model for higher valuation. The preparation to franchise often increases the value of the business even prior to selling the first franchises. The real benefit is creating a valuable chain while simultaneously passing the baton to the next generation of true owners who will enhance and grow the existing model for the retiring owner.

*Adding Distribution Channels*

A few of my clients have little or no retail experience. However, they own factories, fisheries, or other product-producing companies for which they wish to open additional outlets of distribution, to increase and/or stabilize sales growth. If they take a large chunk of capital to invest in stores, they might destabilize their core businesses, diverting capital from an already-winning formula. Franchising can result in hundreds of new sales locations with comparatively minimal investment in store design, franchise development, and legal framework, compared to sinking millions into unwanted infrastructure.

## The Big If

From this point forward, I am going to assume you have a franchise-able business to replicate. This means that you have run your specific business with success, compared your model to the rest of the market, studied the national or international markets in your genre intensely, and concluded that your business is worth cloning.

Here are some characteristics to look for in yourself before you consider franchising.

### *People Orientation*

Are you a good teacher? Are there people on your team or in your life who can train the new franchisees to at least the same level as your existing staff? Is that level good enough to run an entire unit or area?

It is all about the people at the end of the day. It is also about *you*. If you are the most effective, brilliant, and heavily exposed rock-star manager of your empire, and people gravitate to you for that reason, then how is that going to play in other locations? The business needs to be run *without you*, using your system. You must provide and rely upon perfectly executed training and support of your franchisees—who will, I promise you, be starved for information, especially in the beginning. Are your operations manuals and training materials in stellar shape? Is your system simple enough to train dozens of people to maintain the integrity and profitability of your units?

*Management Skills*

You may be the absolute best unit-level manager, but can you manage the team that will be responsible for franchising your concept?

Not everyone can build a franchise chain. Many who are outstanding unit managers should replace themselves as director of franchise. So, know thyself. If you are willing to listen and learn as you go, franchise management can be the most rewarding process imaginable. If you are better at nurturing one unit at a molecular level and this is how you are wired, do not make yourself miserable by trying to be a wide-scale trainer and manager.

*Nurturing Ability*

A franchisor succeeds only if their franchisees are happy and productive.

This is the part that many successful business owners get wrong. Believe it or not, there are a lot of successful people out there who cannot even hold a meaningful conversation, much less teach their methods to the starving minds of new owners.

A would-be franchisor's spirit is just as important as their talent. Do you care about other's success? Getting involved with franchisees is like building a family. Caring about the success of each family member is crucial. Your chain will not succeed unless you nurture every link. If you do not want others to win, do not get into the franchise business. It is not all about you.

*Resources for Initial Investment*

It is imperative that you have strong consulting and legal representation. This investment should be approximately the same amount that you would pay a high-level vice president or industry expert to work for you for a year's time. For that investment, you can score an entire team of experts-in-category to take you through the full development of your franchise and be there for you consistently during the process.

This is the thought process to use when considering building your initial development: What is the value of time? Furthermore, what is the cost of making crucial mistakes at the beginning of building your franchise business?

I am often asked by entrepreneurs in the digital era why they cannot just write their own plans, use their own lawyers, and build their own operations documents. The reason is that the world has changed. Indeed, many boilerplate operations documents could work just fine on their own. The issue is that the documents involved in consulting, paperwork, legal, market intelligence, marketing, *and* operations all need to talk to each other.

The most expensive day in your franchise journey will happen when you fail to hire industry expertise, hire the wrong entity, or outsource so much of the process that you wind up with a pile of disconnected garbage. The team that works for you should be constantly available to you on an ongoing, long-term basis. Work teams that just fall apart after a project are not good for the franchise development process.

A disconnected or inconsistent team may work just fine if you are a computer software developer or even a general contractor on a brick building. But you cannot afford inconsistency in a multifaceted franchise development that requires day-to-day information, updates, and professional advice in multiple categories, and for which the phases and pieces are intrinsically connected.

Pay the right industry experts and experienced attorneys, have them help you build the rest of the team properly, and specify and minimize your ongoing costs for marketing and maintaining your new system. Talent and people are the starting ingredients for ultimate success in this industry. If your experts cannot assist you in all phases of your development in a very connected fashion, then you need to get new experts and network the components together more tightly.

Having said that, your business is your business. I am going to take you step by step through the journey of franchising your business, pausing only momentarily to clarify key definitions, explain changes in the franchise environment, and other staples. How you customize each phase for your needs and knowledge will determine the success of your franchise launch more than anything else.

Talent matters. Do not settle for anything less than the best industry advisors, trainers, and operations specialists prior to jumping in with both feet.

# CHAPTER 2

# WHAT EXACTLY IS A FRANCHISE?

The legal definition and governance of a franchise in the US is handled federally by the Federal Trade Commission (FTC). It is also dominated by separate and important state laws that you must comply with. Layering in forms and requirements are the federal Uniform Franchise Disclosure Document requirement and the sales contracts (generally completed together by your counsel) as you begin to sell franchises.

There are two distinct types of franchises.

- Business Format Franchise: Format franchising is the entire focus of this book. It involves franchising a business of any type according to the guidelines set forth below.
- Product Distribution Franchise: These are licenses to market a product. They are not discussed in this book, as we are focused on perfecting and replicating full business models.

**Federal Law**

Under the FTC Franchise Rule, there are three elements of a franchise:

1. *Trademark*: The franchisee is given the right to distribute goods and services that bear the franchisor's trademark, service mark, trade name, logo, or other commercial symbol.
2. *Significant Control or Assistance*: The franchisor has significant control of or provides significant assistance to the franchisee's

method of operation. Examples of significant control or assistance include:

- approval of the site
- requirements for site design or appearance
- designated hours of operation
- specified production techniques
- required accounting practices
- required participation in promotional campaigns
- training programs
- provision of an operations manual

3. *Required Payment*: The franchisee is required to pay the franchisor (or an affiliate of the franchisor) at least five hundred dollars either before or within six months after opening for business. Required payments include any payments the franchisee makes to the franchisor for the right to be a franchisee. These include franchise fees, royalties, training fees, payments for services, and payments from the sale of products (unless reasonable amounts are sold at bona fide wholesale prices).

If all three elements are present, then the relationship qualifies as a franchise for purposes of the FTC Franchise Rule.

An important point: many new would-be franchisors ask why they cannot simply call themselves licensees and save themselves the hassle of the franchise process. The answer is quite obvious if you read the guidelines above. If it looks, acts, legally controls, and operates like a franchise, it is legally a franchise. The bodies of franchisors who do not abide by both the federal laws and their state's unique laws are piled very high. If you really have more of a licensing distribution concept, then the same law firms who are assisting you in building franchise documents can assist you in licensing instead.

**State Law**

Definitions of franchises under state law vary, but there are several common themes.

In twelve states, the three elements of the legal definition of a franchise are:

- *Marketing Plan*: The franchisee is granted the right to engage in the business of offering, selling, or distributing goods or services under a marketing plan or system substantially prescribed by the franchisor.
- *Association with Trademark*: The operation of the franchisee's business is substantially associated with the franchisor's trademark, trade name, service mark, etc.
- *Required Fee*: The franchisee is required to pay a fee, directly or indirectly.

These states are California, Illinois, Indiana, Iowa, Maryland, Michigan, North Dakota, Oregon, Rhode Island, Virginia, Washington, and Wisconsin.

In five states—Hawaii, Minnesota, Mississippi, Nebraska, and South Dakota—the three elements of the legal definition of a franchise are:

- *Trademark License*: The franchisee is granted the right to engage in the business of offering, selling, or distributing goods or services using the franchisor's trademark, trade name, service mark, etc.
- *Community of Interest*: The franchisor and franchisee have a community of interest in the marketing of goods or services.
- *Required Fee*: The franchisee is required to pay a fee, directly or indirectly.

In Connecticut, Missouri, New York, and New Jersey, the definition of a franchise involves some but not all of the elements enumerated in these seventeen states. Arkansas, Delaware, and Florida have unique filing requirements that are not prohibitive but can better be researched in-depth online on the state's website.

Franchise filing requirements are broken up into three types:

1. *Filing States*: Filing states require the fulfillment of forms and signatures from the franchising entity but do not typically require a full financial disclosure.
2. *Full Registration States*: These states have more in-depth legal requirements beyond the Uniform Franchise Disclosure Documents (FDD) the FTC requires to meet federal requirements. Financial disclosure is required.
3. *Non-Registration and Non-Filing States*: Twenty-three states fall into the first two categories. The remaining US states do not have additional requirements beyond the UFDD and other normal business filings.

Fees charged by each state administrator vary. The state franchise requirement list provided in appendix A is subject to frequent changes but should provide a good general overview of budgeting for the states your new franchise is targeting.

## Franchising Yesterday and Today

Determining when the first franchise was instituted is the basis of some debate. Industry experts will cite everything from use-of-land rights issued by British lords to the Catholic Church's wildly diverse business assets, both nonprofit and for-profit.

For our purposes, the first applicable model-of-type in the United States was started by Isaac Singer of the world-famous Singer Sewing

Machine Company in the early 1850s. Singer had made significant design improvements in the sewing machine. But he could not get momentum in the market due to the training required for the machine's use. In addition, he was close to running out of money to cover manufacturing costs. He needed to create a new revenue model to feed the factory.

Charging licensees a territory tax based on the geographical sales opportunity, Singer was suddenly able to train an army of overworked seamstresses, accomplishing both goals with the new operating capital.

There was not a lot of what we would recognize as pure franchising on any real scale until after World War II. Then a milkshake salesman from Chicago named Ray Kroc received a monstrous order for multiheaded shake mixers from the McDonald brothers in San Bernardino, California. It was so unusual for a hamburger restaurant to produce that much product that Kroc personally went to the store to investigate. Kroc signed up to sell license agreements for the company and eventually bought it out in 1961. McDonald's currently has more than thirty thousand units worldwide.

Today franchise output in the United States exceeds $900 billion, generated by more than 800,000 establishments representing more than 9.1 million jobs. More than three thousand brands drive this monster engine of commerce.

In the early days of modern franchising, it was very much like the wild west. People were buying a lot of thin air. Many con men were raking in loads of cash with very little regulation to counter their efforts. Operational legislation was crucial for this new business form to survive legitimately.

In 1960 an industry group was formed that dominates franchise communication and marketing ethics to this day. It is called the International Franchise Association (IFA). This group provided guidance to the FCC in tailoring the UFOC, or Uniform Franchise Operating Circular, released in 1978. A more refined document, the UFDD, the Uniform Franchise Disclosure Document, was released in 2007. After 1978, federal requirements were much more manageable and consistent.

## Modern Updates to State and Federal Franchise Law

There have been many significant changes in the franchise industry over recent years. Some of these tell a cautionary tale to new or aspiring franchisors as to how the currently strong and dynamic franchise industry will survive.

The most recent changes occurred in 2015, when the National Labor Relations Board ruled 3 to 2 to change the definition of the word "employer." Rewriting laws and changing definitions are short-sighted and irresponsible when they create confusion and upset what has historically been a fully defined and stable set of rules. Such changes make the average restaurant or service business harder to responsibly operate.

Other changes in the larger franchise environment have been made in the legal requirements protecting franchisees. More than 80 percent of franchisees (or their representation) have demanded changes to Item 19—the portion of the UFDD that covers financial performance of the franchisor's existing units. Item 19 financial disclosure has been around since the UFOC was promulgated in 1978, but the fact that franchisees are asking for more hard data to influence their due diligence has wildly affected marketing efforts in the last ten years. This is ultimately a positive development as the franchisee becomes more knowledgeable and uses better access to data in their favor.

We live in a data-driven world. Franchisees have the right to go into your concept with their eyes wide open as to how current units are performing, even if how the franchisor's units are performing is not necessarily indicative of the way franchisees' units would perform with the same model.

The UFDD should be reviewed and updated annually, and the franchisor entity is audited every single year. Although not legally required, it is highly desirable to provide transparency about how units are performing by making full financial disclosure of unit performance available using Item 19.

If you are charging your Rolls-Royce payments to your current parent company, an adjusted Item 19 can be prepared by your C.P.A. to show what does not apply to the franchisee. This gives the franchisee a more balanced profit and loss description. Hiding unit performance behind a wall simply does not work anymore. This fact can be especially troublesome to a new franchisor who is literally building a franchise model from the ground up. The franchisor may not have enough data to please a franchisee candidate due to lack of proof of concept.

Does this mean that a potential franchise buyer should run away from a fantastic new creation because it has not yet scaled in its market? The answer must be based on an individual buyer's goals, methods, and risk tolerance. Some of the most successful franchisees got their start by taking a risk on a newly designed model that had not yet been proven. The key is to line up the right kind of buyer with the right kind of franchisor—one who does not lie, cheat, or steal when representing the sale and process.

Some of the most dramatic changes can be seen in day-to-day franchise marketing. As recently as the 1990s, nondigital advertising venues such as trade shows were full of interested buyers. Much more was in print form or other internet-free methods. Today we live in a universe driven by public relations and social media, all dispersed digitally.

You would think that the digital marketing revolution would minimize expensive marketing costs. Social media, websites, podcasts, and other inexpensive outlets are firmly established. To a large degree, they have rationalized advertising expenses.

At the same time, separating oneself from the pack requires making a lot of noise in the right direction. There are simply too many marketing methods vying for potential-franchisees' attention. Therefore, franchisor marketing plans—and marketing support to assist franchisees at unit level—are crucial to navigating this maze of available media.

Creative marketing is a must in this environment. Old-fashioned franchise trade shows, while very crucial to franchise marketing still today, have lower attendance as a percentage of market size every year. The mix of your marketing efforts combined with the creativity of your planners must be measured and updated constantly, both for franchise sales, and unit-level franchisee marketing.

Last but not least on the short list of franchise evolutionary examples are the expectations of the modern franchisee. Assisting new franchisees in operating with your system and support comes with a grab bag of high expectations, some reasonable and some potentially ridiculous. It is not enough to build a great brand and give another person the right to own a unit and use your system. Royalties must be earned by exemplary systems, support, and coaching on an ongoing basis.

We live in a very litigious society. Amid a veritable fog of regulations, we have to support happy franchisees without our franchisor entity getting sued out of existence. Lawsuits often result from allowing a firecracker into a pile of dry leaves—that is, through poor screening of franchisee candidates.

Although I have written an entire section on acquiring the right franchisees for your brand and model, nothing will stop the downward slide if you do not have, first, training and support systems automated and in place, and second, the correct stewards of those systems to complete franchisee training, store visits, audits, and coaching.

Remember my earlier comment about your ability to manage a chain of support? You might need to do this with a small staff in the genesis of your franchise creation. As you build your system and require more support, be very careful in selecting staff, interview methods, and screening software for franchisee selection.

Franchisor companies can be very profitable and payrolls very reasonable in proportion to their profitability once a chain begins to scale. But high-quality training and coaching can cost serious money before those profits are realized. This is where most franchisors make large mistakes in masterminding their system architecture. Screening for the correct franchisee candidates and training and supporting the franchisees you choose should be treated as key tasks in your journey.

Many additional evolutions exist in franchising, ranging from changes in real estate and geotargeting to the impact of labor laws and insurance. This book is focused on how to franchise *today*. I strive to take the franchise phases pertinent to any business model and customize the development architecture for modern times. History is important when we think about business models and distribution models. But so is evolution.

# CHAPTER 3

# THE FUTURE OF FRANCHISING

Will franchising still be relevant in a world of artificial intelligence (AI) and robotic automation?

Soon our automobiles will not require drivers. Tesla, Ford, Mercedes, and every other important automaker are laying the groundwork for this. Our appliances currently have complete conversations with us (and each other) and are getting to the point where they can cook for us according to verbal commands. AI is poised to solve myriad problems in decision-making at all levels. Automation is being positioned to replace half of the US workforce, including teachers and lawyers.

How do all these radical changes affect the decision whether to utilize the franchise distribution model to scale your business?

Some of my clients in the franchise world find it hard to understand why I ask them to listen to podcasts and television interviews that deal predominantly with new technology companies and Silicon Valley start-ups. I often recommend that they listen to the podcast *This Week in Startups* with host Jason Calacanis, a Silicon Valley angel investor and reporter who interviews the CEOs and changemakers of nearly every new or improved technology that comes on the block.

You do not need to be directly involved in the tech world to keep up with the latest automation that applies to your business. Listening to a consolidated menu of seriously relevant technology is a must for any business owner, especially one seeking to reduce labor costs or add other efficiencies to their prototype or model.

Another thing that surprises some of our new clients happens when we hold our three-day franchise boot camps in Los Angeles or Santa Barbara. Before speaking about franchise market studies and related research, I give all of them free books from the *Freakonomics* series and have them download author and reporter Stephen Dubner and economist Steve Levitt's podcast, which is focused on microeconomics and a search for truth in our decision-making and thought processes.

Of course, it seems illogical at first. Despite all the franchise-specific magazines, books, blogs, and articles out there, I insist on getting a room full of very busy people hooked on a technology investment podcast and an economics podcast. However, the franchisors of the future who will win big will be the ones who are the best informed and best guided before they make decisions.

Lack of preparation for the upcoming brave new world—defined as failure to take advantage of modern automation, intelligence, labor-saving technology, and AI technology—is a recipe for failure in a business. The data-driven world we live in does not include a safety zone for franchise concepts in any industry.

There are sushi machines at some well-known stores that can roll rice better than a sushi chef. I recently visited the National Restaurant Association show, held annually at McCormick Place in Chicago, where I was served a perfect cappuccino by a robot. Not only does this open an important discussion about the future of labor for the workers of the world, but it impacts future franchising efforts.

Franchising at the end of the day is a system of marketing, sales, and distribution. Whether your favorite espresso is served by a human or an android, the name of your company, the branding of your offerings, the system governing your operations, and the royalties paid by your franchisees will all have similar intrinsic value.

The beauty of using franchising as a system is that it drastically reduces the need for capital to open more locations. Opening an automated business is still going to require capital, regardless of the labor structure or the software that takes in the revenue and records it. This capital will be provided by humans, notwithstanding how labor, transportation, delivery, purchasing, and fulfillment are rationalized in the future.

Jobs will be eliminated due to higher wage requirements. It will be necessary to automate positions that would otherwise destroy the potential return on investment for many types of franchise models. However, opportunities will also be created for self-employed individuals to acquire more automated and affordable franchise systems.

As more people become under- or unemployed, many will turn to franchising to buy themselves jobs. They will do this by utilizing Small Business Administration loans, family loans, loans against 401(k) plans, and hard-earned savings.

Compared to other industries, franchising has historically held up quite well in recessions and other downturns in the economy. This will become even more visible when workers are replaced by machines and need to acquire jobs. Franchising will be an attractive option among the limited alternatives in the labor market.

Countless articles, books, and newscasts have emphasized the millions of Americans who work at home as self-employed gig workers. The same mindset applies to underemployed retail and factory workers. Such workers will soon become highly motivated franchisee prospects for skillful franchisors. Low-cost, highly automated franchise system designs will become even more important as existing labor is replaced by automation.

Currently, the world is in a transition period. Most of the labor force is still largely human, but the next decade will see more change in job creation and task shifts than at any other time in our history.

For a savvy businessperson with a terrific brand and model to scale, this creates an exciting opportunity to design a platform that positively exploits this evolution and turns what is potentially a very negative experience into a benefit for workers who need to graduate from or migrate to a new working system.

In 2020, as the COVID-19 virus swept the world, 20 percent of our client base situated in the restaurant industry came to us for automation consulting as part of their broader franchise consulting needs. As a result, we added engineers highly qualified in automation and design to help all types of clients to adapt to labor shortages and wage increases.

It isn't about replacing all possible employees with robots and machines. Much of designing or updating today's franchise involves kitchen automation, labor-reducing software, and a host of robotic and virtual tools to make existing models fully viable in the brave new economy. This applies not just to restaurant franchises, but to cleaning companies, painters, and a host of other service businesses.

Franchising is here to stay. Lobbying efforts from various franchising associations, combined with more forward-thinking international leadership, should slowly rationalize and improve the outlook for this system of sales, marketing, and distribution. It is both the job and the duty of existing franchisors and new franchisors to navigate the new age of AI and robotic automation as it applies to their business models. It will affect every stakeholder at every level of the franchise economy.

# CHAPTER 4

# DESIGNING THE FRANCHISE VERSION OF YOUR BUSINESS MODEL

In the same way that all the pieces of the franchise development puzzle need to "talk to" the other pieces of your development, it is critical that you religiously adhere to a consistent design, branding scheme, and overall message to achieve the desired brand continuity and system continuity sought by successful franchisors.

Although there will always be some unavoidable variations in franchise models when adapting your system to an available space, enough elasticity should be preplanned and programmed into the design to maintain the overall image and presentation of your offering.

If you are a service business providing rug cleaning and floor polishing, having your work van covered with tasteful logos and advertising can be crucial to getting more work. Seeing that van day in and day out will gradually create a comfort zone for customers wishing to use the service. A coffee shop with national name recognition will often adapt to unusual settings by maintaining the logos on their cups, furniture choices, and wall art that represent the atmosphere of their brand.

As entrepreneurs we love to talk about our businesses more than life itself. If given the opportunity, any one of you could tie up a dinner table for nine hours just by being asked the right set of questions about your creation. This is the level of passion my consultancy looks for in franchisor candidates who are anticipating scaling their business. However, there is one trait among business owners and system-builders that can sometimes be unprofitable or unhealthy: susceptibility to flattery. We love to be told our baby is beautiful and that our creation is ready for prime time.

When you are going large, there is more to think about when defining visual details such as the architectural and material design of your store, van, or office. Just as your overall business system must be adaptable to the franchise marketplace, the face of your business must be as well.

This is not costly or problematic when you have a weight-loss office in Los Angeles that has less than ten thousand dollars' worth of logos and interior decor neatly wrapped in one small box. What if you have four Mexican restaurants that each look completely different and have little or no brand identity? You will need to invest a substantial amount of money in procuring a standard store design adaptable to multiple locations, spaces, and sizes.

I estimate that we tell 30 percent of franchisor prospects that building out a franchise with their existing design structure will not be satisfactory, and that updated modelling must be added to their to-do list early in their development calendar. They may have the perfect system, strong staff, solid training methods, and a simple menu, all presented in an atmosphere that took years to create. They just need critical brand definition and architecture prior to sharing their creation with the world.

Adapting a model to a multi-unit offering requires looking at every van, every table, and every user experience. Design is so critical, it can literally make all the difference in the success or failure of an otherwise-deserving, fully replicable business model. Design *matters*, even for simple concepts with very few moving parts.

In addition, the literature and advertising about your services—menus, flyers, letterhead, and so on—all need to be cohesive with your store design. Sending different messages causes nothing but market confusion. The tally of marketing dollars wasted due to mixed messaging mistakes is very large.

The model you create needs to be adaptable to the areas you are franchising. It also needs to be consistent over all of your materials, advertising, and operational methodology. Store design, vehicle wrap, office structure, and uniforms must reflect the business consistently across multiple platforms. Consistent branding may seem boring or unnecessary to some people including many customers looking for unique experiences. However, the systemic value of consistency far outweighs the fickle appeal of novelty that plagues far-flung, disparate units with poor branding continuity. That is why there is a McDonald's the size of a small castle in Times Square, and why Dubai has become a new franchise center. Each has learned to fully exploit franchise branding, franchise loyalty, and franchise consistency.

The most expensive unit location, service vehicle, or taco stand a business owner will build is the first one. The reasons for this are obvious to anyone who has more than three or four locations: everything is more expensive when purchased for the first time. The job of a franchise designer is not simply to act as the architect of your model and make it beautiful. It is also to take into consideration the availability and quality of materials, recognizing which materials will scale, be readily available, and be cost-effective in all the geographies being developed.

Many of the people I encounter or work with every day have designed amazing, beautiful, and sometimes downright flamboyant first openings of a store or service business. If that works for the model and image, that is terrific. However, when scaling the beautiful model to go large, one must consider every nail, board, tile, and shelf as well as every truck, van, desk, and painting. Every detail must be accounted for. Material costs, shipping costs, and availability matter. No scenario can be taken for granted.

If your candy shop requires a fifteen-thousand-dollar custom chocolate maker that is only available from a closet-size factory in Dubuque, Iowa, that can become very scary if you need to order fifty units. If a physical item is crucial to your business, part of the job of the architect or builder involved is to responsibly source all relevant items—not just the tile and brick, but anything that could impede turnkey build anywhere, domestically or internationally.

There is nothing I love more than a perfectly executed design. Being replicable does not have to mean being ugly or bland. Consistency is not divorced from beauty or originality. Once the creatives have made the baby beautiful, make sure that the franchise version of your model is rational for every market you plan to address. Design should be systematically aligned with how your goods and services are provided.

# CHAPTER 5

# BRANDING YOUR BABY

Naming a new franchise model is very difficult. There are billion-dollar companies that fail at this endeavor regularly. How can a new franchisor create a brand, logos, messaging, and mission statement that send all the right vibes and are acceptable and loved across every market they are selling into? Are the existing name and message strong enough to scale today? Should you develop a name internally or hire an outside rebranding agency to contour your face to the world?

Everyone has strengths and weaknesses. If you are a new soon-to-be-franchisor and you have the creative talent to pick a brand name that will hold up across multiple geographies, look great to multiple customers, message well on social media, and meld with taglines and advertising complexities, *go for it*! I encourage you to use your creativity and derive all the joy that comes from it. However, if this is not your skill set, it is time to engage with a branding specialist to introduce your system to the world.

There are many cases in which internal branding has been wildly successful, especially for companies that employ a host of creatives. Even if you are very good at naming things, researching a new brand internally can lack a certain amount of objectivity.

When it comes to branding, your opinion is not the key factor. Customer response is a much more important consideration. This sounds very reasonable, but you would be surprised how attached some people get to a brand they've invented, no matter who tells them that it will not work in the real world. Take a step back and let the experts have a go at it. You lack the objectivity to assess how your offering is visualized by the larger audience.

One of the greatest things about being a person with a lot of experience in franchising is that I have made pretty much every possible mistake multiple times. Some of the most embarrassing of these errors have been ones you would expect; picking the incorrect franchisee to award a franchise to, picking the wrong advertising method, and miscalculating costs on a phase or a project. The hardest thing I have had to learn is probably the most obvious thing to most people: get the branding right before you roll out your first franchise. Engaging in marketing efforts before you have defined your brand is not wise.

Many new franchisors are 100 percent convinced that their cool name will scale the same way in Austin, Texas, as it does in Santa Barbara, California. Sometimes it does. Too often it doesn't. The easiest thing in the world for me to do with these clients is to go along with their non-scalable brand and let them figure out the truth later in the process—but that would be as unethical as it is lazy. I could get on a project faster by telling them their model is beautiful, but it will likely not result in a good outcome for the new franchisor.

Brand is hard to adjust in the later stages. It is so important to advertising and messaging efforts that the energy of the development process needs to focus on getting branding right prior to scaling.

## What to Expect from a Branding Company

**This section is contributed from Steve Brazell, one of American's most sought-after Brand Strategists and Reputation Crisis Managers and the founder of Hitman Inc., Competition Removal®."

### *Building a Brand*

Building and defining a brand is both easier and harder than ever before. Technology and new resources have dropped the cost of launching a business by nearly 90 percent over the last decade. And the market has responded—there are literally millions of new start-ups launched every year around the world. Today, there is more noise in the market than at any other time in history, and it's become more difficult to stand out and be noticed. If you are able to capture someone's attention, on average you have less than seven seconds to share your message. *Forbes* says that more than 90 percent of all start-ups fail. So how can you build a successful brand?

First and most importantly, you need to focus on the problem your business solves in the market. What are your customers' pain points? Are they willing to pay you to solve that problem? The single biggest reason that new brands fail is because the market doesn't perceive a need for their product or service. You must be willing to remove confirmation bias and step into your customers' shoes to ensure that you really solve a problem that matters in the market, whether you are a restaurant model, service model, entertainment model, or any type of model you intend to scale.

Once you've confirmed that you indeed solve a problem that your market is willing to pay for, there are four key customer questions that every successful brand must answer quickly and clearly:

1. What exactly do you do?
2. How do you do it differently than your competitors?
3. How does this benefit me?
4. Why should I believe you?

## *What Exactly Do You Do?*

If your customers and franchisees are going to consider you during the buying process, they have to have a very clear understanding of exactly what you do. This is easier said than done. You must define your category and drive home the most important attributes in that category. Categories and attributes are at the core of how we choose products and services. If you don't have a clear understanding of how categories and attributes work, you may want to hire a brand strategy professional to guide you through this process.

*How Do You Do It Differently than Your Competitors?*

Once a potential customer or potential franchisee understands what you do, you've got to clearly articulate how you are different from your competitors. To do this successfully, you've got to create contrast between you and competing products so that the choice becomes clear. As Steve Jobs said, "It's better to be different than it is to be better." Too many brands fail because they try to tell the market that their product or service is better than their competitors'. But better is usually too hard to measure. People look for products that are different.

*How Does This Benefit Me?*

Don't ever assume that your potential customers understand the benefits of your product. You must clearly walk them through exactly how your product or service benefits them, reduces their pain, or makes their lives better. Remember, your customer is always asking, "What's in it for me?"

*Why Should I Believe You?*

Even if you've been able to stand out, get noticed, and share your message, a potential customer still won't buy your product unless they trust you. Trust is the key to every sale. You must support your claims with reasons to believe, which can include testimonials, white papers, statistics, or the support of influencers, celebrities, and industry professionals.

*A Note on Naming*

Just like categories, names carry attributes. You've got to pick the right name if you want to stand out, get noticed, and be successful. Again, don't just pick a name that you like. Make sure to step into your customers' shoes so that you develop a name that will be resonate best with your market.

Put simply, choose a name that is different. Names don't always have to coincide with your product, service, or industry. The most successful names are often two syllables. Choose a name that is easy to say, spell, and share, and you'll be naming for success.

*Branding Summary*

Building a brand is hard. There are a lot of moving parts you've got to get right if you want to be successful. Stay focused on solving your market's biggest challenges and pain points. Clearly articulate what you do, how you are different, how you benefit the consumer, and why they should believe you. If you do, you'll be headed down the brand road of success.

*When it comes to having a laser focus on branding and messaging, it is always more valuable to listen to those who do it best. We thank Steve Brazell for helping us focus on the branding process.*

\*\*\*

**Methods to Define Your Brand**

There are four categories to consider when picking the ideal name for your scalable brand. These are:

- descriptive
- synthesized
- metaphorical
- hybrid

Descriptive names tend to use keywords that point to a given category, such as Harry's Donuts. They can also be acronyms, riffing off industry terms. Using a founder's name or a geography is also considered descriptive. Examples would be Dell Computer or International Business Machines (IBM).

Synthesized names use made-up words or derivatives of real words to define their function. Examples include Facebook and PagerDuty.

Metaphorical names do not directly describe the business but tap into a feeling or emotion. This can differentiate your brand in your market, and you may wind up defining the market if your business is successful. Examples like Apple, Yahoo, and Virgin come to mind.

A hybrid naming method combines categories, such as descriptive and synthesized or metaphorical and descriptive, to create one unique name. MapQuest is an example of this.

Once the method has been selected, there are various processes to accomplish next:

- category research
- customer analysis
- competitive analysis
- keyword search and analysis
- positioning the platforms in the marketplace
- name generation
- scoring and ranking names
- trademark search and review

Those of my clients over the last three years who have required branding support for their operations have spent anywhere from ten thousand to one hundred and twenty thousand dollars on the process. Some of the big New York firms we have worked with provide many more steps to the process, adding full market testing, studies, and ongoing support beyond the scope of what most clients need with an already well-defined brand and system.

There is nothing wrong with combining the extensive investment of a professional market study with your branding process if you wish to combine the two functions at the beginning of your development. Having said that, most companies do not need to buy an expensive market study if the data they need is already available and relevant.

## Taglines and Jingles

Creating a great tagline for your product or service is even harder than perfecting your elevator pitch. An elevator pitch is a super-short, straight-to-the-point definition of who you are and what you do that takes no longer to describe than a ride between floors on an elevator.

Taglines need to sum up the meaning of your franchise brand in just a few words or a short jingle. Nike has "Just Do It," one of the most effective slogans ever to hit the media, touching millions of motivated athletes and would-be champions. In franchising, think of Taco Bell's "Think Outside the Bun" or Avis Car Rental's "We Try Harder."

The best descriptive style tagline I have ever heard is from Federal Express: "When It Absolutely, positively, has to be there overnight". This tagline carried FedEx into the new age of global couriers and championed their brand.

## Trademarking and Domain Registrations

As if it were not hard enough to deal with who you are and what you sound like to the world, you must also deal with making sure someone else has not already registered the name as a trademark or built a domain around it.

There are several online services and law offices that specialize in taking care of all issues related to trademark law and copyright infringement. Likewise, you need to put the franchise company in the best position when it comes to picking a URL for a website and all the things that go along with your identity, legally and otherwise.

There are hundreds of thousands of registered trademarks and many more domain names and descriptors. At the same time, there are patent and trademark trolls who roam the web, purchasing any name or definition that they think may turn into a company or brand at some point. It pays to have a professional firm brand your business with you and for you. It also pays to have a decent law firm review your chosen name(s) to cover every legality and registration you require.

**Across-the-Board Continuity**

I have talked about having the continuity of branding matched up with the continuity of the franchise business design, whether a logo on a van or a painting on the wall of a medical office. The cross-pollination of your brand across all social, material, event, and showcase locations is vital to your business interests and recognition. You already know who you are, what you do, and what value you provide to the public. Take the time to make certain that the market's perception of all the above is uniquely and carefully thought out before selecting your branding definitions and message.

# CHAPTER 6

# THE FRANCHISE MARKET STUDY—KNOW THY MARKET

In a 2009 interview regarding US wars in the Middle East, former secretary of defense Donald Rumsfeld famously spoke about the known, the known unknowns, and the unknown unknowns. Sometimes it is the hardest thing in the world for entrepreneurial new franchisors to admit that they do not really know the larger national or international market for their product. Nor do they know how their model will perform outside of their existing location. It is always those pesky unknowns that will nuke your franchise if you fail to do your homework.

The homework for today is to ask yourself a very basic question: Do you honestly believe that you have all the data you require to create a successful domestic or international franchise plan?

First, consider the source. What is your basis for wanting to go large and franchise your existing model? Hopefully, as a successful businessperson, you have at the very least visualized your model in other locations and received good research and feedback from a variety of smart people about what a full development would look like. But do you have enough information? How much information is enough information?

If you are intimately familiar with your product or service and how to perform with it locally, you need to chart out and investigate, to the best of your ability, how your model will act remotely. This is a crucial part of the business modeling process. If you need a market study to accomplish this, it should be done prior to any other business plans being developed for the franchise.

There are dozens of franchise models, but the basics of building a responsible franchise market study mirror what any solid marketing firm specializing in this area would do for a major multi-unit company. My philosophy differs wildly from some franchise industry experts when it comes to knowing thy market. It seems to me that, ever since Larry and Sergei invented Google, we put an enormous amount of faith in the information floating around in cyberspace. It's true that much of it is solid gold. At the same time, a lot is outdated, irrelevant, or just plain crap—to say nothing of the new-normal category known as "alternative facts."

Purchasing existing market surveys of your industry is an option, and often a must-do to gather what is "generally known." Typically, however, off-the-shelf market surveys are not completely current, or are not reliable for quantitative hands-on polling of each area of interest. Online industry reports are a fantastic starting point, but would you really want to base the immediate or future development of your brand on them? These reports are what they are intended to be: a broad-spectrum overview of how most nerds in suits think a market is performing, based on a compilation of government and private disclosures.

Unfortunately, I have had less-than-stellar experiences with both government and corporate resources. Always remember: the best information you will get is not tainted in any way by self-interest or the need to push content. The best information you will get is from reliable research professionals with a proven track record of reporting facts directly to companies that pay them for the undiluted truth, and whose incentives are matched with the quality of the facts they provide.

I have no desire for the real world to be that way; it is just the way the world is. Human nature, work deadlines, and misplaced incentives get in the way of the truth all the time.

My philosophy is as follows: if I have a business that is suitable for franchising, and if I have developed a superior system and training approach, and if the economics of the business model are in line, then I am going to do as much research as is practically possible on the market I am entering before I invest significant capital.

This philosophy in no way ensures success, but it certainly lowers the risk of making mistakes. Step outside of yourself and the comfort zone of your existing system to get careful, unadulterated feedback and market data. The consultancy I operate provides market studies for new franchisors and mature companies all over the world. We do this by contracting with teams and having them work with our market intelligence officer. The reason we do not do the qualitative and quantitative data gathering in-house is that the results would be much less effective. Having boots on the ground in the target country or state is much more effective than sending staff out to an unfamiliar territory.

Not every client needs a full market study by any means. Many new franchisors do a tremendous job of learning the domestic and international markets cold. They attend trade shows and industry conferences everywhere, gathering and organizing their data systematically and strategically, and in this way avoid expense at the time they wish to franchise. Every case is different, depending on the difficulty of data acquisition.

Market research can be prohibitively expensive for a new company. Domestic studies that involve a lot of polling or other hands-on qualitative research can cost anywhere from fifty to seventy-five thousand dollars just to investigate a handful of prime regions. International studies can cost significantly more or about the same, depending chiefly on the cost of administrative labor and management expertise in a given country.

## Components of a Franchise Market Study

*Stakeholder In-Depth Interviews*

It is critical that both you as the franchise owner and any team members who will be building the franchise system with you have complete buy-in during the market study process. The investigative team(s) from the agency doing the market study must collaborate efficiently with the key players in the new franchisor organization.

Initially, researchers will seek to acquire a full understanding of the business model and a complete list of concerns from management. This includes franchise-level concerns from industry experts and unit-level concerns among the franchise owners and staff. The researchers will create additional hit lists of dispersed duties and execution items to provide better reporting on the specific study.

Additionally, building the relationship between the research team and the franchise team creates a day-to-day feedback loop of information, moving each process along more carefully and productively as each portion of the study is explored and completed.

*Demographic Assessment and Trend Analysis*

This portion of data gathering is usually referred to as secondary research because, even though it is a primary staple of the study, it is usually completed using current data as opposed to live interviews and polling of individuals and businesses. This process creates the demographic pool that will be used for future demand modeling to analyze your chosen market.

Demographic data used for franchises can include almost any kind of standard data set, but generally involves population age, population market trends, consumer education level, consumer expenditure numbers, and behavioral pattern changes in a specific target audience. Industry-specific trends and foundational data that can be hunted down and verified on the internet or acquired from government sources are also used in this data set.

*Quantitative Survey*

The quantitative survey is a crucial, hands-on part of the process whereby primary data is collected from actual end users of your product in each potential franchise territory. As the name implies, the questions asked of the end users are questions that can be quantified or used in strong data sets to make decisions about actual behavior.

As with most studies, the more feedback acquired, the more accurate the survey. This is called the rule of large numbers. Questions asked will be about current and predicted usage of the franchisor's product or service. The goal is to get the clearest information possible about how the franchisor's business will impact a territory. The survey is the foundation of the demand model for your product.

*Competitive Assessment*

This portion of the study takes into consideration all like competitors in the territory who will impact or be impacted by your franchise. For this data to be of any use, an exhaustive and expansive profile set must be completed on each competitor or potential threat. Qualitative data sets that are not publicly available are constructed by doing "mystery shopper" style interviews, along with interviewing or otherwise acquiring data from existing business owners, competitors, and end users in their natural business habitat. By analyzing competitors from every angle, the researchers will also bring in competitive information about gaps in the products or services offered by the franchisor, which can be fixed if appropriate to the model.

*Demand Model Estimates and Final Study with Recommendations*

Now that the data set is complete, it is time for the research company to create a demand model. The researchers absorb knowledge from each of the previous steps and put together a comprehensive executive summary, along with specific recommendations as to how to approach the targeted market.

The demand model's function is to predict the behavior of end users of the franchisor's product or service by utilizing the live data just accumulated, and to do so within a reasonable margin of error. This is called predictive modeling. It relies in part on intelligent assumptions about facts that cannot be derived from the collected data set.

The best result possible is that critical data indicates "all systems go" for the launch of the franchise. Everyone's eyes are wide open. The new data prevents a would-be franchisor from making a multitude of errors. The worst outcome is that unbiased and highly skilled observers came back with a no-go recommendation based on hard facts previously not understood by the franchisor. This is the reason to do your homework before a substantial amount of money is invested in developing your beautiful model. The model may not function the same way in different business cultures, demand areas, or demographics.

There is no room for prejudice when doing a market study. If I need to strap digital movie cameras to a telephone pole to find out how many women between the ages of forty-seven and fifty-five walk by a specific patch of sidewalk in a specific time frame, I will do exactly that before I will believe the self-interested landlord who tells me the number is seven thousand every Tuesday. The best information is derived from the source. Sometimes it is essential and sometimes it is overkill. Make sure the talent you choose to work with in your endeavor knows the difference.

# CHAPTER 7

# PREPARING A STRATEGIC FRANCHISE DEVELOPMENT PLAN

A properly articulated plan of execution covering each customized phase of franchise development is the heart and soul of a successful launch. Some people make the mistake of thinking that to be functional and successful, the business plan must also be static or unchanging. Like life itself, a functional franchising plan must have the flexibility to absorb new intelligence as it becomes available and evolve carefully with constant updating and nurturing, just like any healthy relationship. Do not think of your plan as a pile of forecasted performance, but rather an evolving success template that is customized by you and for you via your expert team.

The first question you should ask when assembling your plan is who is writing this? There can be one master planner or a combination of several participants in structuring your development plan. I prefer to have an individual consultant in charge of the plan design, and then to have expert contributors in each category.

The purpose of the plan is to outline how your model can successfully fit into the franchise world in a way that is customized for your industry, your team, and your development method. If I am going to build a house from the ground up, I want a builder who has built a few houses before I invite them onto my team.

It always boggles my mind how often new franchisor prospects are perfectly comfortable engaging with people who have never owned a franchise, run a franchise organization, or owned their own business. These would-be experts nevertheless paste a badge on their shirts declaring themselves franchise consultants or franchise coaches simply because they took a seminar.

There is truly no substitute for experience when it comes to franchising and mentorship. If you have not had the train run you over multiple times, you are probably not qualified to be the warning system for a new franchisor who cannot see their own train coming through the tunnel. The person who writes your business plan should not just be someone "familiar" with your industry. The person who writes your plan should be someone who has run a business, executed a successful franchise business or two, and understands the development process, pitfalls and all.

The first move of many franchisor candidates is to call a business law firm or a law firm that specializes in franchising. This is a perfectly logical move considering the level of data exploration that is involved. Certainly it is not the worst move a new player can make. However, while franchise attorneys have their place, it is usually not to be the business planner. Their job is to draft, refine, and execute solid documents. A franchise attorney compiles the UFDD and other franchise agreements that the properly executed business plan defines.

A franchise attorney should not be making decisions about how quickly you should grow, the profile of a good franchisee, the size of the building you will work in, or the way merchandise is sold. An attorney should be given the business plan and read it front to back. They can then customize your legal documents according to the business objective defined by the plan, with the goal of protecting all parties, legally and ethically.

I constantly emphasize that to be successful in the franchise development process, the pieces need to talk to each other. This is not an idle tagline; it is how you accomplish success and continuity in your new development and in your ongoing franchise.

Once you have chosen the lead planner, whether in-house or a consultant, it is time to form the overall team that will be providing the input required for your plan to be optimized.

I have absolutely no respect for a team that would write a plan for a franchisor and then not participate fully in the program as it is being executed. Accountability and incentives are that important.

There can be as many as seven active contributors to developing a plan. Some aspects require outside industry expertise. Others rely on key business owners and managers. Still others depend upon franchise industry experts.

Most franchise industry consultants have historically viewed it as their job to replicate what is already out there, simply using proven franchise development methods to clone what already exists. In short, I find this an incredibly lazy approach. You should not franchise a model without fixing what is flawed in it before you scale. Some things that work wonderfully with a single unit or even a local multi-unit model do not work well at scale. It is important that the talent that builds your plan understands the mission, what areas you are developing into, and how to approach things at both the unit level and the franchise level.

None of this means that you must have twenty-five people working on your plan for it to be a good launch template. What is being accomplished here is the use of an actual real-time situation to embed the successful formula into your brain for gathering the data you need. Ask *all* of the hard questions at every level. Have a plan builder who has run a franchise or worked within the system themselves in a meaningful way.

## What Else Should a Plan Contain?

Assuming you did not do a formal market study prior to building your plan, the plan should at minimum include a thorough market analysis based on readily available information on your industry. A plan should set the table by setting forth the current situation of your model and your industry in a clear, digestible way. Once you have your market description and industry data in logical order, you can move on to the other fundamentals.

## What Franchise Structure Are You Selling?

What is the franchise structure? Are you going to be selling only to sophisticated multi-unit buyers for your first franchisees? Or are you going to allow individual mom-and-pop buyers to get in on the action? How about international licensing or master franchise awards to various countries after you scale domestically? When is it time to develop internationally? Every type of franchise offering requires its own contract.

A conversion franchise in the case of fitness may look like this: Brad owns a gym that is approximately two thousand square feet in Calabasas, California. He has been unsuccessful in attaining profitability with his current model, which lacks the passion and intensity fitness clients demand. Brad is willing to do a complete gym makeover and convert to a superior franchising business model

Since Brad is already in the industry, we offer him a reduced franchisee fee to remodel his gym to our system—if we are consistent in offering other conversion opportunities the same fair deal. Brad and his trainers are thoroughly trained under the new system and replace the old with the new.

This is an ideal conversion scenario and very common. Other models, such as Ace Hardware, built an entire dynasty on converting mom-and-pop stores to their system, putting in superior buying co-ops so they could compete with the Lowes and Home Depots of the world. This model saved the fortunes of literally hundreds of family businesses.

Choosing franchise structure(s) can be a huge decision in and of itself. Some models are built precisely to focus on the individual buyer, whether a work-at-home opportunity, a hobby business, or a body shop. Others only work with area developers with sophisticated teams that can train and have deep pockets to develop more methodically and quickly. To find the right mix of structures for your goals is a key part of team discussions going into a new development.

## Competitive Analysis

When entering the franchise business, you are not only concerned about the competitor down the street. Your main concern is other franchises that may appear more attractive to potential buyers you want to have in your franchise family.

A comparable list of franchisors is an essential part of any franchise plan. In addition to looking at franchise competitors, I always recommend listing multi-unit corporate models that are appropriate and even single-unit businesses that have dangerously good ideas and may show up in a SWOT (strengths, weaknesses, opportunities, threats) analysis as competition. One of Bill Gates's famous quotations is that what kept him up at night was "two guys in a garage in Silicon Valley" as opposed to strong, known businesses.

Even though a strong comparables list is predominantly focused on successful players in the franchise arena, the kid in the garage still matters. and you must stay current on systems that may overpower or outsell yours in the future. Even if they are not yet franchised, be sure to add systemically important threats to your list.

## Staffing the New Franchisor Organization

What talent should you bring in initially for this new company? It is a new company, by the way. Just prior to forming the legal structure, you are going to create at least one new entity and possibly two. The first entity will be the franchise company or corporation. The second will likely be an entity to hold on to your intellectual property. Not every attorney recommends this for every model, but it is common, depending on your operational processes and any secret sauce that makes it work. The talent you decide to hire for your new franchise company may be working for your current organization, or they may be drawn from outside your bubble. In either case, they will be working for the new franchisor company now.

The franchisor entity is not your original entity, but a new container. Its purpose is to pay for the expenses and staffing of the franchise operation, sell franchises, support franchises, and collect royalties. The original company (or companies) is likely going to be listed as an affiliate of the new company. It is important to note that the records and transactions should not be comingled, nor should their separate responsibilities. Earnings and payables for the franchisor organization need to be confined to the proper entity and properly accounted for.

In a new franchisor company, it is completely common and often desirable to utilize talent from the existing parent company. The new company will pay that talent on an as-needed basis to carefully scale the labor and stop it from going out of control prior to revenue being accomplished and rationally budgeted.

Regardless of how you staff the company, insource or outsource, there are few scenarios in which you should pile on payroll in the beginning stages of a franchise company's life, before positions can be financially justified by .franchisor company revenue. There are multiple exceptions to this rule, usually occurring when a larger company is utilizing a franchisor employee in multiple ways to prepare the company for business and needs to accelerate the payroll temporarily. Payroll may go upside down for a while until sales momentum can catch up. As a rule, I prefer to hire only the fundamental positions—starting with sales and support administration, and fundamental marketing mechanisms—until new payroll expenses can be justified.

The ideal starting staff depends largely on your own abilities and the abilities of your existing team. If you are a strong communicator, you may anoint yourself the director of franchise sales and handle all incoming leads, meetings, discovery-day events, orientation, and so on. If you are strong on the operations side but do not feel comfortable with the long and arduous handholding process of selling to franchisees, then you may hire a salesperson almost immediately. The positions you hire first will be the positions you are weak on, not the positions applicable to someone else's organization.

Here is a typical start-up-employment scenario for a reasonably funded new franchisor office:

- *Franchise Director*: This person initially will run all operations and, in many instances, be directly involved in franchise marketing and franchise sales activity until the business scales.

- *Franchise Marketing Director*: The marketing director's tasks include advertising, vendor coordination, public relations coordination, event and trade show marketing, and social networking functions. In a new franchise, this person usually has a second job (dual function) of supporting franchisee marketing efforts. It is not unusual for 40 percent of this person's time to be dedicated to unit-level marketing efforts, depending on the weighted load value between vendor efforts and in-house abilities. Understanding effective lead generation is key to this position.

- *Franchise Salesperson*: This person coordinates CRM (Client Relationship Management Software) management, utilizing leads from the marketing director. They are on top of the long and carefully orchestrated franchise sales cycle of finding and awarding the correct franchisees. This person generally has a relatively low base salary with a high commission rate (subtracted as one of the key expenses covered in the up-front franchise fee when a franchise is sold) and should be from a mindset or industry that understands business sales. Communications from when a lead is generated and recorded to disclosures and discovery days are all coordinated and executed from this position initially. Pre-screening a new lead begins the process, flowing into calls and introductory brochures and other materials to build the relationship with a potential franchisee. The salesperson will be responsible for getting applications properly filled out, conducting or coordinating with management to conduct appropriate background checks and other due diligence as needed, and disclosing the required Uniform Franchise Disclosure Document (UFDD) to the potential participant, allowing at least fourteen days for review prior to engaging in any business or contract activity. The goal of the franchise salesperson is to bring a highly qualified potential franchisee into "discovery" or a "discovery day," during which the prospect joins the franchisor at their location or appropriate training facility to be shown the business "live" and to meet management. It is their opportunity to evaluate your model and everyone in it who is involved in the process or in day-to-day franchise operations.

- *Director of Training and Support*: Support systems for franchisor organizations vary widely in structure. If you are running a series of unit locations, who is responsible for monthly or quarterly store audits and visits? Who is the training director guiding new franchisees through the required phases of learning, whether at headquarters or another training facility? You may have one solid training manager who is leased or otherwise borrowed from the company store, paid on an hourly or project basis, and several other trainers involved in in-house training. Since support requirements are more frequent in the beginning, you may need to hire a full-time support director right away. If your new franchisees are not properly supported in your system, they will slow down, cease royalty payments, or otherwise rebel against your system, poisoning your model for later potential business. In short, you need to get this right. Like all other positions in the new company, the support side is profiled very carefully to balance the load against the system, likely renting bodies from the mother ship until more revenue is achieved.

- *Franchise Administrator*: This is the office coordinator who generally directs traffic between the industry-specific software that runs the entire franchise system, franchisee requirements, and management. Once a franchisee signs the documents and purchases their unit or territory, there is a multitude of tasks to keep on top of, including insurance requirements, labor requirements, local requirements, design requirements, royalty payments, and requisitions. If there are not at least two people trained on the system and software, the franchisees will suffer and so will the business. There is a strong argument for having a full-time person driving the car to coordinate support teams and administrative tasks.

In the beginning, everyone is wearing many hats. The franchisor founder may be the sales director, marketing director, and chief service provider to franchisees in the very early stages. However, full focus is important, and every effort should be made to scale staffing at the correct pace to ensure amazing service to franchisees.

Since franchising covers so many industries and support models, it would take an encyclopedia to convey every option for sales and support structure for a new franchisor organization. This is only a snapshot of what may go into a typical company in the early stages. Additional sales, support, and operations professionals are then phased in based on the average number of franchises opened and forecasted. In many cases, franchise sales brokerages or other third-party sales are layered into the core team to increase lead and scaling volume.

My recommendation is that most starting franchisors should first learn how to develop their own leads and sell their own franchises. They can explore the benefits of broker relationships *after* learning that process. Some simple concepts—such as Play Live, a video game room in various malls and strip centers—use brokers almost exclusively from day one with great success. The reason for this is that their model is very simple, and the brokers utilized are very connected and familiar with the franchise while it is scaling.

Third-party brokers are often distracted. A broker can sell four Subway franchises more easily than they can sell one of your new and unproven units. So are they focused on you? I am a big fan of control and laser focus for my franchisors. But the decision whether to outsource a portion of your sales and marketing depends largely upon the complexity, sales cycle, and demand demographics of your model. The decision needs to be made explicit in the business plan and backed up with solid research, like every other management decision.

Some franchisors utilize third-party brokers as an expensive lead source or meeting generator to get more scale, and that can be a good decision. In this scenario, the internal sales team works very closely with the broker and still carries the majority of the weight and prospect-facing time in the sales process.

A key labor-controlling device is to use superior software to run your operation. FranConnect, Naranga, and other franchise-specific industry software may cost quite a bit of money in monthly fees, but when weighed against the savings you will realize in labor and administrative expenses, such software can be much more cost effective than developing Enterprise Resource Software or Client Relationship Management tools from scratch or piecemeal.

My consultancy has medical and weight-loss models, as well as multiservice franchises that choose to develop and/or customize their own software. This makes perfect sense if you want to own all aspects of your technology for a specific service model. It does not really make much sense if you own a restaurant franchise. Off-the-shelf, franchise-specific software is abundant, and only minor customization is required for an efficient back office. A software cost analysis should be a key ingredient in your strategic business development plan.

## Fees, Royalties, and Other Revenue Generators

The franchise fee should be designed to cover the up-front costs associated with the acquisition and support of new franchisees, including commissions. You may make a little money on the franchise fee too, but that is secondary to covering launch costs.

Many franchisors make the mistake of underpricing the franchise fee, for fear that a realistic fee may inhibit a buyer from acquiring your franchise. Say that you must charge forty thousand dollars to recover your expenses when others are charging thirty-five thousand. If a potential franchisee is making a career commitment to use a brand, system, and royalty structure, and they refuse to pay that difference, then they probably are not a serious buyer or someone you would want in your day-to-day franchise life. Right pricing is the key to fee amounts. It is important enough to deserve its own section in any given franchise plan.

Royalties are the amounts paid weekly or monthly, generally based on gross sales. (There are other structures based on net performance.) Royalties are largely commensurate with the gross margins the business typically earns. A service business cleaning houses is a lot more profitable in terms of gross margin than a restaurant that offers low-margin, high-quality food. The restaurant location may have a royalty on gross revenue of around 3 to 5 percent, whereas the cleaning business might have a royalty of 6, 8, or even 10 percent, depending on its margins and the support provided by the franchisor.

There is no single standard royalty for any industry, although my consultancy does list the royalty of every known competitor when we do a competitive analysis (comparables) to come up with some basis for discussion. The factors considered when establishing a royalty rate are what the market will bear, the average margin of the business, any premium qualities that suggest a higher value, and the overall service load for the concept—that is, what the franchisor will spend to properly support the franchisees.

You do not want to take advantage of your franchisees or put them in a position where they cannot make money. As Jim Kramer from CNBC's *Mad Money* likes to say, "Pigs get slaughtered." Make sure your up-front franchise fee and your ongoing royalty percentage make sense competitively and in terms of keeping your franchisor company profitable.

However, always consider the value you bring in service and support to the franchisees from their perspective. Without them, you have nothing.

In addition to the royalty revenue, your model may generate other revenue from franchisee purchases of products or services from the franchisor. An example of this is Sadkhin Therapy, one of our clients based in New York City. They have a weight loss and lifestyle program designed for a variety of overweight challenges, some very extreme. Their program employs dietary and scientific techniques. They carry their own line of health products, teas, and supplements that is completely proprietary and a key part of the revenue model.

Refresh Companies in Ohio specializes in refurbishing key household spaces such as bathrooms and kitchens. Their four franchises specialize in refinishing, painting, carpet cleaning, and janitorial services. Refresh carries its own private-label line of refinishing chemicals to ensure compliance with their strict guidelines. These products also create an additional revenue stream for their organization.

## Pro Forma

Once you have defined every profit center, franchisee expectation, franchisor expectation, development estimate, budget, and all other factors involved in the launch of your new franchise company, you then need to lay it out in a three- or five-year pro forma to easily visualize your economic goals in the most realistic terms possible.

There are two sets of pro forma spreadsheets my consultancy includes in a franchise plan: one reflecting goals and expectations for the franchisor company, and another showing the performance of the franchisee units we intend to sell and support.

This is one of the more illuminating pieces of the puzzle. If you use actual historical data (profit and loss statements, expense summaries, and similar reports) and have done a good job calculating future expenses, a pro forma spreadsheet shines a realistic light on the potential of your model.

Most of the number-crunching entrepreneurs whom I work with skip over anything brilliant we create in the text of the business plan and go right to the pro forma, memorizing the key assumptions before going back to the written descriptions. There is no wrong way to read a business plan if you absorb all the facts and assumptions.

One of the remarkable things about franchise business plans is how little they are properly utilized. Everyone uses their plan to strategize in the beginning, which is indeed its core function. It is important to build the plan, if for no other reason than to organize your thoughts and the economics of what you are asking other parties to buy in to.

Famous trader, analyst, and author Nassim Nicholas Taleb writes in his book *Skin in the Game* that he puts very little stock in a document such as a business plan. I respectfully disagree. But I will meet him halfway by saying that most business plans are underutilized. They are perceived, falsely, to have a sense of finality when you need to be nimble, constantly pivoting as new information becomes available. In other words, a business plan needs to be a *living, breathing document* that you actually use as a tool.

To Mr. Taleb's point, all the crafting and goal-setting in the world only tee up your process. The *execution* of your franchise plan is the real challenge. No matter what level of genius writes your plan, you will find yourself pivoting, flexing, and realigning your goals with every new activity and learning experience of your journey. The plan is just a terrific road map. Make the map expertly, update it constantly, and keep it as usable and simple as possible.

The last thing I would like to leave you with on the initial planning side is this: the goal is to have realistic expectations and to build a fairly conservative outlook into your planning in most cases. Be aggressive in your sales and support efforts and outperform your realistic plan, but do not overforecast to the point where goals are unattainable. It takes serious time to build your franchise family. Gauge how long your model needs to grow, and pace it carefully.

# CHAPTER 8

# PREPARATION OF FRANCHISE LEGAL DOCUMENTS

---

Now that your strategic franchise business plan document has been assimilated and perfected, it is time to create the franchise entity or entities and to prepare the Uniform Franchise Disclosure Documents (UFDD), complete with inserted franchise agreements for the structures you are selling.

It is vital to find great franchise legal representation that can expertly assemble all your franchise documents, represent you legally (including in litigation, if needed), and protect your trademarks and other intellectual property. It is also important that legal and administrative mechanisms are responsibly in place, either insourced or outsourced, to handle annual registrations, insurance issues, and any other legal requirements associated with franchisee training, obligations, and government-required functions for compliance. If you are dealing with one of the larger firms specializing in franchise law, you may be able to keep everything under one roof.

Regardless of how you separate or consolidate the legal talent hired, it is very important that the legal team takes the time to understand your business plan and to study all pertinent data carefully. They should send you a questionnaire to solidify all information about your current organization. If you don't hire an attorney who specializes in franchising and understands the myriad potential challenges, you are making a fatal mistake right off the bat. Many new franchisors get mixed up with inadequate counsel. Or they scrounge the world for boilerplate documents to try to save money.

Either way, they wind up lacking the customization, ongoing legal support, and safety that come with crafting a solid document set.

Looking into the track record of an attorney who specializes in franchising is more important than ever. A popular attorney who attends all International Franchise Association events and is a darling of the industry recently got sued for tens of millions of dollars for neglecting his responsibilities to franchisors. Strangely, he is still around today. If you do not have a good industry consultant to advise you on what firms to use, please take the time to investigate your counsel carefully.

Although not required, I personally prefer attorneys who are both good drafters of documents and experienced litigators who have represented franchisees *and* franchisors. There is no substitute for experience, whether in running a franchise business or in drafting franchise documents. Little is worse than missing items in a franchise contract due to a lack of focus or experience on the part of the attorney.

I have seen contract templates that were so outdated, they had Roman numerals for version numbers. You need an attorney who has a clear understanding of the industry and keeps current on all new legislation. They should also take a preventative approach to labor issues and other hot buttons that are changing in this industry. Such hot buttons may open litigation problems in states that are not business-friendly.

**What Kind of Entity Should I Be?**

The kind of limited liability company, C corporation, S corporation, or even B corporation that you should create as the franchise entity depends largely on your personal tax structure needs as well as your operating method within those needs. There are at least two parties you should consult prior to making this decision. The first is your certified public accountant, or CPA. If you do not have a reliable and savvy CPA, then get a recommendation from your attorney. A CPA should be able to assist you in deciding the best structure for the franchisor company. The other individual to consult is your franchise attorney.

For purposes of simplicity, I am not going to go into the mechanics of the amazing companies that are creating new corporate structures for social responsibility and giving back, such as benefit (B) corporations and Limited Liability giving structures. However, if you are looking to add this level of social responsibility to your franchisor mission, your attorney can investigate and create these structures for you.

The following are the most common legal structures used by franchisor entities:

- *C Corporation*. A corporation is a separate legal entity set up under state law that protects shareholder assets from creditor claims. "Shareholders" in most cases are limited to the founder(s) of the business—the term "shareholder" does not imply that shares are publicly traded or held by outsiders. Incorporating your business automatically makes you a regular or C corporation. A C corporation is a separate taxpaying entity with income and expenses taxed to the corporation, not the shareholders. If corporate profits are then distributed to shareholders as dividends, those shareholders must pay personal income tax on the distribution, creating double taxation. Many small businesses do not opt for C corporations because of this tax feature.

- *S Corporation*. Once you have incorporated, you can elect S corporation status by filing a form with the IRS and with your state, if applicable. Profits, losses, and other tax items pass through an S corporation to the business owner and are reported on a personal tax return (the S corporation does not pay tax).

- *Limited Liability Company (LLC)*. Another business type that is formed under state law and gives your personal liability protection is the LLC. Taxwise, an LLC is like an S corporation, with business income and expenses reported on the personal tax return. If you are the only owner of an LLC, you are viewed as a disregarded entity. This means you report the LLC's income and expenses on Schedule C of Form 1040, the same schedule used by sole proprietors.

On top of the usual tax considerations, you also should discuss with your attorney the ramifications of adding investors, whether initially or in the future, to the franchisor entity. You may elect to go with a traditional C corporation if there are multiple investors. Or you may elect to divide units from an LLC to decide profit disbursement when distributions are made.

## Building the UFDD and Appropriate Franchise Agreements

When you sell a franchise, you must fully disclose the current situation, risks, and management background of the entity doing the franchising. You must also disclose any required affiliate activity, which describes at a minimum the relationship between the parent company and the new franchise entity.

The laws governing these rules are listed under Rule 436 of the FTC code.

## Franchise Rule Summary

The Franchise Rule gives prospective purchasers of franchises the material information they need in order to weigh the risks and benefits of such an investment. The rule requires franchisors to provide all potential franchisees with a disclosure document containing twenty-three specific items of information about the offered franchise, its officers, and other franchisees.

The UFDD must be disclosed to the purchasing franchisee fourteen calendar days prior to any agreement. Accepting payment or executing the agreement prior to the waiting period will not only void the transaction but set the franchisor up for serious litigation.

The following sample table of contents of a recent UFDD shows the twenty-three items required to comply with Rule 436. It will give you an idea of the depth of information required about the franchisor entity, its management, and any past lawsuits or pending litigation.

Once the disclosure portion is completed by your franchise attorney, you will build and customize the contracts you will be selling franchises with, called the franchise agreement(s). As mentioned, not every franchise offers every contract structure. The following is a list of US and international agreements and their definitions:

- *Individual Franchise Agreement*: In an individual franchise agreement, a franchisor grants a franchisee one franchise unit within an area of primary responsibility or defined territory.
- *Area Development Agreement (Multi-Unit)*: In an area development agreement, a franchisor grants a franchisee two or more franchise units within an area of primary responsibility or defined territory.
- *Subfranchise Agreement*: In a subfranchise agreement, a franchisor grants to the franchisee the right to exercise powers normally reserved exclusively for the franchisor within a specific territory. The rights granted in a subfranchise agreement typically include the right to offer and sell franchises; the right to collect fees and royalties, with some split percentage going to each (shared percentages are typically determined by the training and support provided by either party); and the right to provide training services and support to franchisees within the subfranchisee's designated territory.
- *Master Franchise Agreement*: In a master franchise agreement, a franchisor grants a master franchisee the right to own and operate more than one unit and the right to subfranchise the right to open units to other franchisees, all for a specified time and within a specific area.
- *International Licensing Agreement*: In an international licensing agreement, a licensor grants the licensee the right to produce and

sell goods, apply a brand name or trademark, or use patented technology owned by the licensor. In exchange, the licensee usually submits to a series of conditions with respect the use of the licensor's property and agrees to make recurring payments for that use.

- *Conversion Agreement*: In a conversion agreement, a franchisor grants an established business in the same industry the right to convert their independent business into a franchise business by contracting with the franchisor organization. Once the conversion agreement is signed, the established business is required to conform to all the franchise requirements. It is no longer known by its former name, but now follows the branding and systems of the franchise.

## Permission to Use Your Brand (Internal Licensing Agreement)

The company you based your franchise on is now an *affiliate* of the new franchisor entity. Who owns the name, the brand, and the intellectual property?

The next thing you need to do is gain permission to use your own name and system. A separate licensing agreement is usually made up between your existing entity and the franchisor entity. This gives the franchisor entity the right to use the name, trademarks, system, advertising materials, and marketing materials your existing entity developed. All the general and proprietary items that the franchisor company requires to operate are included. The agreement usually runs for several years.

## Forming an Intellectual Property Holding Company

An intellectual property holding company is not always required or recommended. However, a franchise attorney who handles licenses, trademarks, and other intellectual property may recommend forming a separate holding company to keep these items away from the franchisor entity. This is not guaranteed to prevent litigation, but it does add another layer of separation that would need to be pierced in the case of a serious lawsuit or disagreement.

**Required Individual State Filings and Registrations**

The following is a consolidated version of the attachment shown in chapter 2 that outlines every state requirement for all registration and filing states. This chart shows what your administrator or your lawyer will provide each of these state entities, including but not limited to the application, the salespeople authorized to participate in the sales process, the UFDD, and any advertising materials requiring viewing or approval.

Once your law firm finalizes the FDD, they will complete and file, on your behalf, state-specific and state-required franchise registration applications. The law firm will complete the applications with information provided by you. You are responsible for paying the requisite state filing and registration fees and postage. You are also responsible for submitting the completed applications and providing supplementary materials to each state's regulatory agency.

Supplementary and supporting materials for the franchise registration application typically include, but are not limited to:

- The Uniform Franchise Registration Application
- The Supplemental Information Form
- The Salesperson Disclosure Form
- The Uniform Consent to Service of Process
- The Corporate Acknowledgement and Certification Page
- The Franchise Disclosure Document
- Franchisor Advertising Materials

| Registration and Filing States | | | |
|---|---|---|---|
| California | ☐ | New York | ☐ |
| Connecticut | ☐ | North Carolina | ☐ |
| Florida | ☐ | North Dakota | ☐ |
| Hawaii | ☐ | Rhode Island | ☐ |
| Kentucky | ☐ | South Carolina | ☐ |
| Illinois | ☐ | South Dakota | ☐ |
| Indiana | ☐ | Texas | ☐ |
| Maine | ☐ | Utah | ☐ |
| Maryland | ☐ | Virginia | ☐ |
| Michigan | ☐ | Washington | ☐ |
| Minnesota | ☐ | Wisconsin | ☐ |
| Nebraska | ☐ | | |

**The Value of Time**

Let's pretend that you have just completed your UFDD, franchise agreements, and state registrations and are getting ready to sell franchises. Do you really want to spend all your time filling out forms, tracking multiple items from multiple states, and keeping yourself in compliance?

If you do not have a highly qualified administrator who is good at these tasks and can keep all the balls in the air for you, then you should probably seek an agreement with your law firm to handle registrations and related communications. To make this possible for my clients in the consulting world, I arrange with our most trusted law firm to provide flat-rate annual registration management at a low cost. Their paralegals and admins handle the bulk of the work. Franchisors should be focused on sales and support, creating happy franchisees and training them as much as possible. Do not hesitate to outsource registration and filing functions responsibly.

There are a multitude of additional operational tasks, such as annual updates and audits, insurance policies, and general compliance.

Therefore, there is no scenario in which a rock-solid franchise software and management system would not be fully utilized. If you choose to outsource certain functions to reduce labor and maximize your time, you still have to manage administrative activities efficiently and at a low relative cost.

### Which Franchise Types Should You Use for Your Offering?

At the bare minimum, franchisors will prepare the UFDD and a single-unit franchise agreement. If you want to sell multiple franchises to developers wanting to commit to multiple locations, then you also include a multi-unit or area development agreement.

### What Are the Mechanics of an Area Development Agreement?

Although the way development contracts are designed varies wildly, an area development agreement essentially works like this:

- You have an area development contract. The obligation of the franchisee is to purchase a specified number of units within a territory (say five for this example) and open them for business within a specified period (say five units over five years, or one unit every twelve months).
- The franchisee signs the area development agreement.
- The franchisee agrees to the standard single-unit agreement, representing the first unit only, and pays the franchise fee in its entirety for this unit. Let us say the franchise fee is thirty thousand dollars per unit. After the fourteen-day waiting period, one check is written for thirty thousand dollars.
- For units two through five, a second check is written for whatever percentage is negotiated of the balance of the area development agreement. Let's say that percentage is 50 percent. The second

check would be for thirty thousand dollars times the four remaining units times 50 percent: $120,000 x 50% = $60,000.

- As each of the remaining four units opens year after year, the balance on each unit—fifteen thousand dollars apiece—is paid when the individual agreement for each location is executed.

Some franchisors offer a franchise agreement that requires payment for the entire development up front. Others offer a variety of payment options and percentages. The important thing is to be consistent and make sure that you ask for enough to handle your franchisor obligations, such as initial training, support, and marketing expenses.

If the franchisee does not fulfill their obligation, some franchisors keep the amount paid up front and do not refund it. How you plan to treat these matters will be explicitly asked by your attorney prior to document completion. Different franchisors have very different philosophies as to how to treat a default or cancellation due to nonperformance.

Many franchisors only want to deal with sophisticated franchise developers and do not do single-unit agreements at all. Examples include Moe's Southwest Grill, Crushed Red, and Five Guys Hamburgers. These franchisors do not have to suffer as many issues as inexperienced (or less-well-capitalized) individual franchisees can create. Many franchising experts are reporting that this is the way the entire industry is leaning. I believe there are always going to be models that perform fabulously by offering single-unit entrepreneurs the ability to control their own destiny.

What about going international? Will your concept work as well or better in Dubai or Japan than in the US and Canada? Have you tested your model in a foreign market? Personally, I feel much safer opening a few corporate stores in a foreign market prior to engaging with franchisees, if this is possible. Alternatively, the franchisor could sell a Master Franchise Agreement to a very experienced and well-funded local developer. Selling something you cannot measure or support properly is risky at best.

Keep in mind that franchise brands and demand for their offerings are wildly different. You cannot simply stand on one argument and not drill down into the needs of each franchisor individually. Doing a market study is great preliminary work, but there is no substitute for testing an area live before asking a franchisee to take a risk on your offering in an unfamiliar geography.

## Automating the Contracting Process

The sales process and compliance issues can all work together nicely if you utilize the right software system to run your company and carefully train your salespeople about waiting periods, rules on claims and liabilities, and all other legal and ethical requirements. The International Franchise Association (IFA) has some terrific videos. I recommend that all franchisors join this organization. Members should require their salespeople to watch and take notes on all the sessions, whether live at a franchise training event or online.

IFA certifications are available, and I likewise strongly encourage them not just for salespeople, but for everyone involved in the operations of a franchisor organization. A certification for a franchise expert is called a CFE.

In some scenarios, having gone through these courses and certifications will add credibility to your organization. Certainly the information will help safeguard the franchisor from many common errors that arise from a lack of understanding of the rules of selling and supporting franchises.

Industry-specific franchise software will allow you to send a UFDD to the correct state in the correct form automatically. The salesperson must have the discipline to follow the fourteen-day waiting period before contract execution. Most reputable software packages automate the delivery of franchise disclosure and contract issuance right in their core modules. Alternatively, you can have your law firm do a courier-return envelope for signature on the closing date or do a closing meeting in person. Always set rock-solid systems up for compliance many weeks prior to the sales process commencing so all federal and state-specific franchise requirements are followed at all times.

This section's focus is about drafting contracts, complying with legal requirements, and choosing structure. We will go into greater detail on franchise marketing tactics, franchise sales, and the important discovery day methodologies when the client visits your concept up close.

## When Would I Use Subfranchising?

Subfranchising is a type of area development agreement that goes far beyond simply allowing the franchisee to buy multiple units in a territory. In an area development agreement, the franchisor is still responsible for selling the franchises as usual—and, more importantly, supporting the franchisees with its immediate staff. A subfranchise model is an area development agreement in which the franchisee takes the place of a franchisor. The subfranchising franchisee sells franchises for that territory and provides either full support or a predetermined level of support that the franchisor would normally handle on its own.

This method of franchising can be very useful in a lot of situations. Recently we had a client who did not have a presence in the state of Florida but had a developer there who could sell to a lot of existing relationships and obtain commitments much faster than the franchisor could. This enabled the parent franchisor to add an additional twenty-unit commitment in less than one year and guaranteed a great team to do both on-site monthly audits and routine daily support.

In this type of arrangement, the subfranchisor generally makes the lion's share of the royalty payments, but the split between the parties is negotiable or different for different industries. The sub may take 70 percent or even 80 percent of the royalty, leaving the franchisor with a much smaller percentage of revenue. However, it is better to have 20 percent of something than 100 percent of nothing, especially if a reliable party is supporting your brand in an unfamiliar territory.

## Master Franchise Agreements

As described above, a master franchise agreement acts very much like a subfranchise agreement. If you are trying to put your model into Saudi Arabia and you do not know the culture, speak the language, or have the business connections to do anything beyond basic marketing, it would certainly behoove you to have a seasoned partner with development experience as a franchisee. The master franchisee subfranchises from the parent franchisor, with a percentage split of royalties proportional to their service. A 90/10 or 80/20 agreement is not uncommon, as the master franchisee is doing everything in-country, with only logistical and remote support from the franchisor brand.

The best rule of thumb for subfranchising, master franchising, and various flavors of international licensing is that the percentages shared is balanced in proportion to the amount of support weighted on the franchisee or subfranchisee versus the originating franchisor. This can be a rewarding and lucrative way to enter multiple markets as your franchise brand develops. I encourage you to investigate the economics of this after you have a solid, well-run domestic development to see if setting goals worldwide is a wise progression.

# CHAPTER 9

# OPERATIONS AND TRAINING— MANUALS, MATERIALS, AND RECOMMENDED PROCEDURES

꘎꘎꘎꘎꘎

This chapter's focus is the importance of having a seasoned operations consultant with a solid team behind them to put your exact operating methods in writing and in practice for your franchisees. The operations consultant should also create a program whereby everything from location geotargeting to unit-level support are defined and executed. Your goal is to run and teach the best system in a constant, consistently updated motion. Each moving part of your operation should be well oiled and improving every day.

The benefit of taking the time and expense to update an entire operations manual frequently—for example, every two years—is not always self-evident. A properly run franchise updates each section of their operations manual as needed and should have a cloud-based, pass-coded system where this data is stored and kept current. But a big difference exists between routinely updating sections of a manual and pulling your entire franchise management team together to rebuild the defining guide from the bottom up.

Purposely punching up your main manual forces each department, employee, and profit center to be examined and updated as a cohesive group. Often the review increases the efficiencies and profitability of the franchise company. It also resolves inaccuracies and communications problems for managers and crew.

We are living in an age when methods within our structures change so rapidly that each moving part must be examined for improvement at the corporate and unit level in a constant and disciplined way. You will find that a seasoned operations consultant is a great resource for building your initial manuals and training materials—or at least for organizing them if you have a seasoned training staff and materials already. The templates used to define the most efficient operations methods when a company is new are also useful for targeting bottlenecks and inefficiencies when a system is mature.

An operations manual is the *nucleus* of your operating methods, definitions, and training materials. Most of the training materials, manuals, and forms for daily use will spawn from this original document set. A solid operations consultant needs to be wired in such a way that they can visit your company, review each method of operation, and document it comprehensively in a teachable form.

Typically, the operations consultant does not define what you do or how you do it. That is not their focus, although efficiency improvements and suggestions about method are a critical part of the defining process. The job of the operations consultant is to focus on and define what you are doing in such a way that, say, when you are in your kitchen creating your proprietary laser-fractured, oven-fried Twinkies, and you stir the batter with your left hand while simultaneously pointing the laser into the bowl with your right hand, the timing, machine settings, magic mix of ingredients, and vivid picture of all the above are meticulously documented and simple for the reader to absorb and execute.

The operations manual for your franchise is intended to be used at the unit level by the franchisee, the franchisee's managers, and appropriate employees who are authorized to view it. It is not a document to be set out for everyone to take home with them. Specific training materials for wider disbursement will be derived from this master document, such as technical directives for a service business or a recipe guide for a restaurant franchise.

The operations manual should be kept under lock and key or digitally pass coded if cloud based. Although every business utilizes different levels of technology, the ability to access procedures, recipes, descriptions, onboarding procedures, and routine forms through a computer or smartphone should be provided. Who has access and how the manual data is distributed should be clearly defined to all levels of management in the organization. Cloud-based software companies that specialize in digitizing and distributing entire training regimens, such as Tovuti or Trainual, are excellent resources for creating a paperless, fully secure distribution method.

## Qualifying Your Operations Consultant

There are many managers who are distinctly talented at organizing and building operations manuals because they have spent enough time implementing procedures for their businesses. They understand the best layout in their category or categories. They know how to incorporate compliance requirements into day-to-day operation. Many of my clients are franchising small restaurant chains, and we often send in former multi-unit location managers who are now consulting for our firm to build those manuals, taking advantage of their management execution experience at the unit level and their consulting experience in defining the layout of the contents.

As in many other industries, it is skill set more than work history that we focus on when picking the best person to replicate and define processes. Sometimes new franchisors get confused as to the type of seasoning and experience an individual or a company should have to be qualified to build franchise operations and procedures.

The operations person who writes your manual and documents your procedures should not be a smart teenager on summer vacation who has a knack for writing and organization. The operations manual builder should be a seasoned technician who has built a wide variety of programs for multiple business types and who is laser accurate in their descriptions. The seasoning is as important as the talent. You need both.

No shortage of young talent exists. Eventually these young people will make excellent operations consultants. But you need to physically have been through the process numerous times before you know how to incorporate all the nuances, efficiencies, and legalities into someone's core structure. Farming out this task to a generic technical writer with little or no experience in the franchise industry is sloppy and irresponsible. There are many little things in a franchise business that can be bootstrapped or economized on effectively. Defining your system is not one of them.

There are insurance requirements, tax requirements, OSHA workplace requirements, and procedures for picking and opening locations. A well-rounded manual writer who is not from the franchise industry does not have the background to nail all this down—not because of a lack of skills or intelligence, but because of a lack of experience and seasoning.

As you may imagine, the process of absorbing all a franchisor does and how they do it takes more than one casual on-site visit. When our consulting firm sets up operations procedures, we first do a long conference with the new franchisor. We set them up with questionnaires and industry-specific templates we will use for their operation.

It is important for super-busy business owners to know that, after the setup procedures specific to them are completed, a highly trained operations consultant is basically going to be living with them for the next week or two, depending on the complexity of the operation being defined.

If the operations consultant is building a manual and notices a lot of inefficiencies, this is a great time to sort out system changes with the business owners. We often see beautiful business models that need serious changes. We recommend and perform a separate efficiency study and process review prior to building the manual and defining the structure.

A good franchise consulting team is also a business consulting team to a large degree. Make sure the team and the operations consultant you bring on have the history and talent to assist you in improving your operations while also documenting them.

## Master Table of Contents—A Simple Sample

This book is not intended to be used directly to build your templates for plans, operations manuals, or other materials. Each company and franchise operation is unique in how their manuals should be built and how each heading and requirement should be annotated.

Having said that, I think it would be productive to give the reader a basic snapshot of how massive and detailed these compilations are and the level of detail you must record in them. Remember, most of the detail in an operations manual is customized to run your business, and much of it covers regulatory and legal requirements. If you print one out, do not be surprised if it is four to six inches thick for even a simple business.

My company, Franchise Science, is quite different from other consulting firms in that we spend a lot more time perfecting the unit-level business prior to franchising. We work with our own designers as well as experienced contractors who aim to perfect the franchise design in cases where that is needed or desired.

We recently did an operations manual for a traditional family pizza unit location. Our design department devised three separate franchise models for it. Therefore our assigned operations consultant needed to define operations for three models.

The sample in appendix B mentions pizza places, but it is the master table of contents we started with prior to customization. I have displayed this so you have an instant visual of the categories that comprise a manual. Some of the sections have been purposely eliminated to maintain client confidentiality. As you read the sample table, imagine what a table customized for your business might look like.

Did I mention that this pizza business did not require a particularly complicated manual? There are many pieces, and each facet of the plan needs to be examined, defined, and documented. Efficiencies that are not up to par in any category should be fixed at the corporate and unit level before a franchisee is exposed to the system, not after.

I have arguments with other industry experts who wish to sell their legal or consulting services and depend 100 percent on the new franchisor to identify the readiness of the operation all by themselves. People miss things. It is part and parcel of a good consultant's job to look for problems in the business model and operation and to suggest and/or implement solutions. Yes, it *is* the responsibility of the franchisor to perfect their operation as much as reasonably possible prior to selling franchises. It is the consultant's responsibility to identify leaks in the plumbing before the franchisor goes live.

When one of our clients was searching for a franchise consulting firm, she was told by one of our competitors that the franchise operations manual was not a big deal, and that the consultants would not even need to go to a unit location to gather data. Our team lived on location for seven straight days. Later, we flew back and rerecorded updated procedures prior to documenting them. Building those manuals, putting them in the cloud, describing all the technicalities of the business, and final editing took sixty days. Do you really think that the consultant who never went on location would have done a good job of cloning their operation? How would you like to be the first franchisee to have to use that consultant's manual? How could such a manual possibly make all the pieces fit?

Everything matters when you are training franchisees to work within your system and to evolve with you as activities change. The category template you use needs to be appropriate to your model, but the entire manual needs to be customized to your system.

Many people, especially zealous new entrepreneurs on a tight budget, think that templates are the solution to everything. Templates can be great. They just do not apply to the hard part of the job, which is having the talent to execute and document each phase in the best way.

If you put two hot dog stands next to each other and examine their procedures thoroughly, you will find out very quickly that even if the end product is similar, the vendors' procedures for getting it to you are wildly different and very much worth noting. Your method is your method. Do not have someone build your system who does not know franchising, operations, and compliance simultaneously. You are not a widget on an assembly line. You are documenting how you execute your creation, your intellectual property, your methods, and your brand.

## Who Actually Uses This Monstrosity? Pick a Cloud. Save a Tree.

If you do what most people do, which is run your business and only use the operations documentation sparingly or in training-material form, then you can be proud to say you are one of the 98 percent of American managers who are in the same boat. However, the information for every purpose—including legal protection and defining processes—needs to be utilized.

Training is the most crucial thing for developing franchisees and customers' brand experience. Making it easy to access systemic data is crucial in the information age and can make all the difference in the world to new trainees and needy managers. They need guidance when they are following guidelines for opening a new location, meeting insurance or other state-mandated requirements, or responding when someone slips and falls on their floor.

The modern way to ensure massive utilization of operations documentation and training materials is smart software. The quality of a company's software has a direct correlation to the quality of life and the quality of work. Nobody in modern times should have to search through four inches of your business bible to find the answer to a question.

Smart software is most likely to take the form of a cloud-based operations platform that automates all the accepted search procedures of any smartphone or computer to immediately acquire the data a store manager or franchisee needs.

Features of these platforms will vary along with their names. The system should have the entire manual loaded into it and be formatted for quick access to any form, procedure, or topic. A few frequently used features are:

- new location opening requirements
- store visits (unit inspections) and audits
- survey forms and audit results
- new employee online onboarding
- job descriptions and duties, including daily punch lists
- training materials, including online testing and handbooks
- frequently used forms
- field consultant information and mentors
- daily updates and memos
- supply order screen (if not already on another system)
- shift schedules (if not already on another system)
- emergency contact list
- recipes and portioning (for restaurant models)
- marketing methods and requirements
- new product or new service approval procedures

## Franchisee Training Materials and Testing

Many organizations and small businesses have very proficient trainers and managers who not only get the brand's message and procedures across but are very good at preparing presentations and materials. For instance, if you come from a well-funded, fully staffed company with terrific materials, you may also have an ideal teacher to prepare them. In that case you should prepare materials in conjunction with an operations manual update and do it in-house.

Most of our clients do not start out with significant staff or resources internally. So creating and packaging the franchisee training materials is done in sync with the operations manual itself. Information is disseminated from the operations manual. Presentations and handbooks are made and testing materials are created.

For most franchises, there are at least two levels or phases of training. Phase one is the new franchisee going to your headquarters or dedicated training location and participating in on-the-job training (OJT). The trainee is shown how to do every oil change or brew every cup of coffee. Every operation from the back of the house to the point of sale is learned thoroughly.

During phase one, some number of prespecified training hours are required. These are listed in the UFDD alongside the tasks to be completed and tested on. Although training materials are updated far more often than operations manuals, the first time around, the two should be done in tandem.

Phase two training is when the franchisee is getting ready to open their own unit. At this point (depending on the model and training requirements), it is typical for the franchisor's on-site trainer to assist the franchisee for several days or weeks to ensure a successful launch.

Some businesses only have one phase of training. Some have four phases or more. Regardless of the system, everything must be defined and illustrated in the most simple and digestible form for the new franchisee and staff.

**Ongoing Education and Related Materials**

How often should you get together with your franchisees for group meetings and training sessions? Who pays the tab when annual meetings are held?

The operations manual describes everything in detail, including ongoing education requirements. Most franchisor companies have annual meetings or other events to get everybody into a room for socializing, networking, and training. Materials for such occasions should be prepared well in advance and cover topics most important to the franchisor and the franchisees in the most current form.

A lot of franchisors, especially those who are new and have just spent a substantial amount of money on initial development, do not think it is important to hold events in the early years. Nothing could be further from the truth. Even if you have the simplest of business models, building a cohesive team means doing a live event at least once per year.

Some things need a real human connection. This is hard for some folks to understand in an age of drone delivery and AI. It may not make perfect business sense, but the level of connection and support from networking your team in person is a must.

Franchisees, contractually speaking, should pay their own travel and hotel expenses to attend these meetings. The franchisor can cover the meeting room or office expenses related to the event. Although there are low-cost, high-tech models that do not do this or require this contractually, I believe even today something is lost when you do not connect live at least once per year as a franchise team.

## Building a Support Team

Assembling the best people to train and support franchisees represents another crucial set of decisions for the franchisor who is aiming for excellence.

In the beginning, the support team may look a lot like the sales team—which happens to be you. The busiest and most challenging time in a new franchisor's life is generally the early stage, prior to multiple units having been sold. The reason for this is that royalties coming in from a handful of units cannot justify the ideal payroll required to babysit *your customers*—who are the franchisees.

The franchisee does not work for you. The franchisee needs to work *with* you and to feel the positive energy and practical benefit of your franchisor support system. A system does not require having three hundred people on call, but it does require excellent execution from the few who are needed.

Each model is wildly different, whether in cost, design, how it scales, where it scales, or the cost of proper training and support. When you first sold the franchise to a prospect, you either built enough revenue into your upfront franchise fee to cover initial training and opening costs, or you included a separate price list of franchisee-absorbed costs.

Before the franchisee is in place, you need to define how often you or your field representative is going to get out to see them, how long you will spend with them, and who pays for what. In the UFDD, the responsibilities of both parties are described. If the franchisor pays their own way to visit the franchisee (common for audits and reviews), then that must be listed and signed off on with everything else in the franchisee's contract and UFDD disclosures.

When my consultancy is first looking at franchising a new model, we do a comparative study of similar models. One of the first things we look for is the competing concept's support system and how it is supported and maintained financially. Most commonly, the franchisor is charging enough in royalties to maintain their support system and office employees while making a good profit. Just remember that when you set up your travel and support system, every dollar spent and whose responsibility it is to spend it must be carefully defined and described. If you didn't figure this out when you were running the numbers in your strategic franchise plan pro forma, then you didn't do it right.

Before I discuss the ideal profile of a trainer or field rep, let me first interject that when you are a franchisor who needs to support franchises, it is generally a lot better (depending on the technology and methods involved in the support model) to have your franchises clustered together and saturating a complete market. If you sell franchises one at a time all over the place, your support costs are going to be overwhelming, and you will not profit from the experience. There are some exceptions to this rule. For example, a low-cost business model (from a support standpoint) uses an opportunistic strategy or a demand-based strategy instead of creating a defined matrix of where new units are to be saturated based on location, demographics, overall demand, and other factors.

## Training and Support Personnel Profiles

As mentioned previously, a franchisor manager or employee, especially in a new franchise, is going to be wearing a lot of hats.

If you are the franchisor and you are a gifted relationship builder, salesperson, and communicator, then you may put on the hat to handle the overall sales process. Perhaps you will hire a marketing director to generate leads while you manage the franchisee database and connect with the initial prospects. Or perhaps you are the operational genius and think you are more suited for training and support mastery, while you hire a more gifted sales professional or organization to assist you.

Regardless, the people involved in your initial training and ongoing support processes are likely to handle phase one and phase two training with you and for you. As the franchise scales and royalties increase, so do the number of positions.

Whoever your best trainers are, you need to make certain that they stay on point and on script. I am in no way saying that their unique personalities should not be able to shine. This is what the prescreening and vetting processes are for—so that you can remove the sarcastic and the serial killers from consideration. Those who remain should be people you can trust. You need to take the same level of precaution with background checks on your training candidates that you do with vetting new franchisees. The same testing companies that create the software for vetting CEOs and franchisees also have a questionnaire for training staff. Background checks, vetting, and measuring camaraderie and relationship-building skills are vital.

I have personally encountered situations in which some of the most talented trainers in a category were fine in a classroom setting or doing on-the-job training but had soon-to-be-discovered drug problems or alcohol abuse issues. If a trainer representing your brand goes completely off the rails, it will likely reflect on your business and people's view of your hiring practices.

Surprises in the hiring process are not completely avoidable. In this, they are like any other risk in business. However, you must use the technology available to limit the risk as much as possible. You seek a team player, a long-term relationship builder, a great learner, and an outstanding teacher, along with a persistent helper with high energy and loads of integrity.

Once again, it is all about the talent. You know the ideal way to run your business and the ideal training methods for a given unit. Hopefully you have a team in place, and the ideal training partner and field representative is already working for you in some capacity. If not, make sure that your vetting process includes more than just a résumé and a reference check. Utilize today's hiring software and take your potential trainer(s) on a long test drive in-house before launching them out to the franchisee network.

## Online versus On-Site Visits

Many franchise models, including some in the food category, are easy to support using technology, webinars, and cameras to replace on-site visits. I argue these should be relied on to a limited degree.

To use a personal example, I own a consulting firm. Since most of our work product consists of conversations and written materials, what purpose would it serve for me to fly out to Latvia or Dubuque, Iowa, to visit consultants or planners who work for me? It is not practical for me to do very much in the way of travel for our internal meetings, except for annual meetings in Santa Barbara, California. I live on airplanes to take care of clients. Therefore, my business model does not require monthly, quarterly, or annual on-site visits of my offices to maintain quality control.

Say that an oil change company has a pair of trucks performing car and fleet maintenance tasks with a limited inventory of filters, oil, windshield wipers, and so on. How often do the operators need to see you if you are the franchisor/trainer? How often do you need to audit your model and performance in person? Quarterly maybe? Are they going to move the oil pan two more inches to the left after you leave for the airport?

The question needs to be studied. If the on-site needs of the model are low, then you may choose to go with a quarterly visit, giving the franchisee the option to pay for time and travel for impromptu visits to get involved in specific challenges that come up. In this way, you do not create a choke point for special situations but rationalize the regular running system for travel and support commonly needed.

With restaurant locations, fully automated or not, visiting the units monthly or at least quarterly should be the minimum, even for mature models. Technology has been the biggest factor in reducing required visits. It is simple and inexpensive to prepare presentations and training for online tutorials. Franchisors frequently have access to live video via store security systems to check on many potential issues. However, a full store audit requires a human checking the inventory, food preparation, safety, cleanliness, and a range of punch lists and tasks.

Therefore, support methods are not templated across the board. Creating the ideal support structure and choosing what type of technology to use are among the most important decisions you will make in your franchisor organization.

## Franchise Survey and Audit Results

A franchise audit is not a financial audit. The purpose of the franchise audit is chiefly to measure all aspects of compliance and performance with the standards set by the franchisor. Since some of the most detailed audits are done on unit location franchises, let us consider a typical format that you would find on a field representative's tablet. Please turn to appendix C and review the sample outline of a franchise audit reproduced there.

Audit procedures are combined with routine support visits. They are scored internally, and sometimes also externally. The goal is to bring every store up to franchisor standards, performing at a high level.

One of the questions I am frequently asked is "Should we as a franchisor publish these scores on our portal or cloud platform so the franchisees can see how they measure up against other stores?" Having run several retail locations and two franchises myself, my gut always wrenches a little. I remember sitting at regional meetings of Radio Shack back in the 1980s. Our district manager threw out everybody's store performance scores while handing out handmade hat trick awards and other novelty items to celebrate the winners and pound the losers. I still have a closetful of custom-carved hat-trick awards that I refuse to part with, as they represent successful turnarounds of four underperforming stores.

If I am a franchisee being scored, I do want to know how I compare. But do I need everyone else to see my numbers? This is a decision for the franchisor. Many competitive-minded leaders like to put each location's numbers on a board for all to see.

You have the ability technologically to score a unit and immediately compare them to the rest of the chain without revealing individual unit scores. You also can celebrate top performers by showing every franchisee how each store performed—unless it violates rules outlined in your agreements or nondisclosures.

If you have a traditional Item 19 financial disclosure that requires listing the performance of all stores (as opposed to just the healthy ones), eventually everyone is going to know each other's financial performance, if not their audit scores.

Healthy competition among your franchisees is fun and exciting to watch. Pounding a franchisee over the head with poor audit numbers creates a losing situation, making recovery much harder for both parties.

Instead, use the poor-scoring franchisee as a trigger to spend more time training. Get out to their location quickly and with a well-thought-out solution. More money is lost by poor management of the franchisee relationship than almost any other function in franchising. You will spend tens of thousands of dollars annually to find the most appropriate franchisees for your system. When human nature creeps in and some of them falter, you can't just sit on the sidelines and bitch. You really need to send a SWAT team in for an effective amount of time to drill down to the best operational solution(s).

When you have identified a franchisee problem or a problem franchisee, be the first one to act and solve the issues. If the franchisee is not qualified and you have made a terrible mistake, then you must measure the audit forms against the franchisee requirements in your contract. If justified, you can then send what is called a notice to cure—or, if warranted, a full termination letter via counsel. This will not happen often if you have chosen wisely in your quest for highly qualified franchisees, but you must be prepared for all instances preemptively.

## Levels of Notice to Cure

In your franchise agreement every enforceable event must be defined, whether minor offenses or immediate termination offenses.

Here is an example of a typical notice to cure situation. A franchisee has a cleaning business. A service van or other vehicle is required by the business model. Upon a recent inspection by the franchisor's field representative, it is found that the vehicle requires engine maintenance, it has not been washed in a month, and the franchisor's logo on the side of the van is invisible. Upon further inspection, it is discovered that the floor-buffing machine needs replacement. Despite the franchisee doing a great job regarding appointments and service, they are not keeping up with equipment and supplies in a timely manner.

The franchisor, upon completing the audit, issues a routine audit report and has the franchisee sign it. All the items in need of repair or replacement are listed, along with a car wash and detailed notes about supplies and the proper method of presenting the company logo.

On the next visit thirty days later, the franchisee has cured all the items and ordered up supplies. They continue to do an outstanding job with appointments and service. The issues are satisfied, and the field representative will keep tabs on the franchisee while offering support in any way possible. Everyone is happy. Lessons were learned. Life marches on.

Alternatively, consider a different franchisee from the same cleaning franchise who came on three months ago and is just getting started. They have been through phase one and phase two training, have worked with some of the franchisor's best people, and seem to be in great shape to start marketing in their area. Prior to signing the contract, they had been thoroughly vetted, undergoing a full background check and taking a highly effective computer quiz on the franchisor's onboarding software. During training, they interacted positively with other trainees and aced every test and OJT function.

Then a strange phone call comes in from the Dubuque police department: the franchisee has just been arrested for selling heroin to teenagers out of the van.

The franchisor does not need thirty days to cure this. The franchisee will be terminated immediately.

It is important to note that not all franchisee problems are as cut and dried as the examples above. Disputes and operating challenges can go on for months. Having properly drafted franchise agreements is essential. Getting franchisees to sign off on offenses found in unit audits is also critical.

You cannot enforce what you do not write down, and you cannot enforce what you cannot prove. Keep your audits in order. Many franchisors treat unit audits like a festive field trip. Camaraderie is wonderful, but you are there on business! Keep your records in order, whether you are using an automated cloud system or old-fashioned manual forms.

A sample notice to cure is shown in appendix D.

## Franchisee Termination

Say that you have done everything possible to fix a franchisee at their location, without sufficient results. You are likely losing money in this lackluster scenario. As in any business model or distribution setup, there are as many problems and solutions for a poor-performing franchise unit as there are stars in the sky. Most of them are minor and can be handled with your excellent support team.

In the franchise agreement, most franchisors insert the right—but not the responsibility—to take over a nonperforming unit that is violating performance standards if that violation is not legally cured over a specified period.

If a location is simply shut down due to noncompliance with no cure, the franchisee must take down all advertising materials, bring the books and royalties owed up to date, and close the business. They are free to open another business in the same location if they have time left on their lease, but not a business that violates the agreement or any noncompete clauses in their contract.

If an ex-franchisee decides to knock off your business and continue operating with all your vendors under a new branding setup, they may well be in violation of trade dress laws or other noncompete requirements. In some states, such as California, it is very difficult to enforce a noncompete agreement, but the franchisee is still subject to other laws protecting the franchisor. Your franchise attorney's job is to go over these scenarios with you as they apply to each state you are selling franchises in.

When the franchisor terminates a franchise agreement and takes over the terminated franchisee's location, the franchisor must take on the burden of properly managing and staffing the struggling location until the franchise can be resold. The lease clause in the franchise agreement must be executed, and the lease is then assumed by the franchisor, along with the monthly payments.

It can be a very difficult situation if a budding franchisor without a lot of extra cash flow is put into a situation where the new and scaling brand is in danger of being tarnished, but the actual unit location is highly desirable if properly managed and maintained. Not only will good revenue be lost by closing the location, the brand is likely have taken a punch or two.

In short, you must do everything you can to build your model out with the right people, the right goals, and the right energy. You also have a responsibility not just to yourself, but to the other franchisees in your chain to adhere to your own standards and to enforce them throughout all units developed.

## Approving a New Location

Whether building out your franchise as individual units, area developments, or a combination of the two, the franchisor has final approval of location. Typically, the operations manual will clearly lay out the criteria for a location and the approval routine. This is fine if you are working with experienced developers who understand traffic patterns and have a high degree of past success in geotargeting locations.

Finding good locations for retail businesses in this day and age can be seriously challenging. After the financial crisis of 2007 to 2009, the markets blew back with a fury. For a while in the US, our money was on fire. Many successful businesses that were less recession-proof went out the hard way, and retail space became more available. This was a very short-lived situation.

One of the most important things my consultancy's design team does is work with realtors all over the country to find spots for retail franchisees. Although the devastating effects of COVID-19 are shaking up the commercial real estate environment, great care must still be taken when identifying the ideal locations for your franchise.

We do not believe much of the information we get in from the real estate community. We are constantly investigating locations and monitoring patterns on behalf of our clients. My advice here is simple: when it comes to locations, make sure the data you get is rock-solid. Measure carefully before you dive into a location.

As a franchisor, make sure your resources are set up so you can carefully investigate a location to ensure your franchisee has greater chances for success. Do not allow a real estate agent to rush you into a bad location or lease negotiation. Build this investigative routine into your costs and methods prior to accepting a location, even if the standards set forth in the franchise agreement and the operations manual are met.

## Insurance Requirements for Store Locations and Vehicles

Picking a responsible insurer for a work vehicle, physical office, or other tangible asset is an important part of operational requirements. What a lot of new franchisors need to be aware of is that not only should you approve a responsible insurer of dependable quality, as your contracts and manuals indicate, but you should also be listed as an additional insured on your franchisee's policies to account for any potential future liabilities.

If a customer is visiting one of your franchise locations and slips on a banana peel, it is very possible that they will sue all the way to the franchisor. Make sure all parties are insured for amounts that make sense for the model. Discuss liability insurance with your attorney and your consultant to make certain you have the right protection at the right cost.

## Personnel and Managing

One of the best things about franchising, as opposed to the burden of opening multiple company-owned units, is that the burden of hiring and managing employees at the unit level shifts to the franchisee.

Most of the operations manual templates that are built by serious operations professionals cover all OSHA requirements, definitions of employee responsibilities, and hiring practices quite nicely. However, neither managers nor employees will make use of documents or other operational materials unless they have simple tools to access information.

Everything from checklists to job boards to time stamps needs to be defined and customized for your business. It is not enough simply to have an employee sign off on their responsibilities with all the dedication and enthusiasm that most of us have when we accept the terms and conditions on free Wi-Fi at Starbucks. Make certain that the franchisees and their management are following procedures carefully when you audit their locations or service businesses.

The franchisee owns the franchise, but you own the brand. The system that is followed must be administered equally, from the lowest employee on the totem pole to the highest-paid manager and the franchisee themselves.

If you have not taken the time to peruse the personnel section in the sample master table of contents (appendix B), please take a moment to do so. Imagine what the ideal descriptions might look like inside of your customized and perfected operations manual.

**Franchisee Unit-Level Marketing and Advertising**

In chapter 10 I will talk about building the ideal unit-level marketing plan for your franchisees to use at their locations and in their territories.

In the operations manual, the marketing plan may be inserted or it may be referred to as an external document. It should be made to show not only all the appropriate marketing options, but the franchise agreement's minimal requirements for contributions to the advertising fund(s).

Example: let us say you have a new fitness club opening in Los Angeles. In your franchise documents, you have built in the following requirements for the franchisee to contribute to the marketing fund as a percentage of gross sales.

*Local Marketing*

The franchisee is required to spend money on local marketing in their own territory at a rate of 2 percent of gross sales. They may be doing local events such as throwing a fitness training party on the beach, where potential clients are invited to join existing ones for a free session and some healthy food. Some of the funds may go to a local newspaper or magazine, although the effectiveness of this method may be limited in the digital age.

Perhaps you are going to hang offers on doors, guerilla style, or send a squad of super-fit messengers to company offices to offer programs. All of this will cost the franchisee time and money. And frankly, for a new fitness location, spending only the 2 percent minimum may be way less than they need to get a base level of customers into the fitness center.

Maybe the plan recommends a 5 percent marketing budget for the first three months after spending a grand opening amount of ten thousand dollars. You can only enforce the 2 percent minimum expenditure (or whatever amount you baked into your franchise agreement), but you can still give some solid tiered options to show your franchisee how to succeed within a reasonable budget.

Local marketing funds are not sent to the franchisor. The franchisee copies the franchisor monthly on receipts showing proof of expenditure in the local category.

*Corporate Marketing*

The franchisor will usually have a marketing fund that is fed by the franchisee(s) and generally is collected into a separate account (single-purpose account) that is used only for advertising materials, digital media, and any other marketing that is spent for the benefit of the entire franchise chain. The franchisor entity or its advertising agency spends the funds for this single purpose, and monies cannot be comingled with other revenue.

It is common for these percentages to be debited from the franchisee to the franchisor's bank on the same day as royalties, but this is not the case with all franchises. Some franchisors take control of all the marketing funds, including local advertising responsibility. This is not usually the case, as the franchisee tends to be more familiar with their local market. It is not unusual for a franchisor to collect 0.5 to 3 percent in advertising fees for a given system. Many models use predominantly local advertising and only require a small contribution (or no contribution) to the franchisor's corporate ad fund. The division of amounts and advertising focus is as diverse as the models in the industry.

## Co-op Funds

A third advertising method included in most franchisor options is cooperative advertising. This gives the franchisor the ability to use the scale of their franchise to negotiate great deals, such as commercials played on a radio station, targeted event planning, or other aggressive media methods, and pay for this with pooled advertising funds collected from franchisees in the affected territory. Although this approach is the least emphasized in food and service models, larger and more sophisticated franchises can benefit in a huge way by cutting ad costs and increasing return on investment (ROI) in each market.

I hope you have been given enough examples of the variety of procedures, methods, protocols, and requirements that need to be buttoned down to create a successful franchise operation. Do not worry—nobody in their right mind does it alone. Taken inch by inch and built with a solid team, both the learning and the execution processes can be enjoyable and fulfilling. Building these pieces and implementing the initial units is the hard part and must be done with a lot of care. Once the carefully constructed machine is humming along, you will find that running a franchisor company is probably easier than the business you are running today.

Today you are the business owner and entrepreneur. You are working all day and half the night. The last time you took a vacation, candy bars cost a quarter. Tomorrow you will be the teacher. The operations in your head will have been systematized into a productive force passed on to carefully selected and nurtured franchisees. Sales and support functions will be divided among a trusted group of managers working in tandem. With proper management, proper documentation, and an iron will to protect and honor your brand, this can be the most rewarding business experience of your life.

# CHAPTER 10

# THE UNIT-LEVEL MARKETING PLAN FOR FRANCHISEES

Some of the greatest business models in the world spend absolutely nothing on marketing. They either have the most desirable products or services with a natural word-of-mouth network, or they simply have been doing a great job for a number of years and people are drawn to them.

Marketing is happening for these amazing models, whether they pay for it in dollars, in time, or in building the natural network.

Your franchisees do not need to compare their marketing needs to your marketing needs after you have proven your core model in your territory over a respectable timeline. They need to get off the ground and they need the smartest unit-level marketing plan for their business with the best ROI they can earn.

When you are a new franchisor, it is very possible that your initial franchisee locations may not have a following of any kind yet. Even if they implement your systems perfectly, your franchisees still need to launch with some momentum and do consistent and effective marketing, both before and after their base is established.

**Effective Marketing Methods for Your Model**

Current marketing methods to build up your franchisees' sales figures need to break through a chaotic sound barrier to be effective. So many voices pummel our computers, televisions, and phones that getting the message out on our product or service has become a science in and of itself.

This is true whether you are a franchisor building a marketing plan to sell individual franchise units, or a franchisee trying to create a unit-level plan to build your location with satisfied customers and happy, evangelizing disciples of your brand.

I call this convoluted mess "the art of noise." How you penetrate the sound barrier and make yourself heard will largely determine the success of your business. Although there is no substitute for an amazing product, we need to be heard, understood, and desired in order to make a successful franchise.

## Public Relations Driving Digital

It probably is not a newsflash to you that a compilation of different types of marketing are required to get people connected to a new franchise. Although there are some standard digital marketing tactics that apply to all geographical areas—such as websites, social media presence, and search engine optimization—unit-level marketing plans should be customized to a specific market area and franchisee budget.

In the previous chapter, I talked about the minimum advertising requirements for a franchisee. Funds must be spent at the local level and the corporate level. In some cases, all the digital and social elements of marketing are handled centrally through the franchisor's marketing department or agency. One of the reasons for this is that if a franchisee can form their own website or social media system without centralized governance, the messaging can and will quickly turn into a runaway train. Lack of common parent-child governance is a recipe for disaster and a tarnished brand.

Sometimes franchisees do not think about this. They create their own local pages and social media accounts without thinking through the system. This is usually the result of a lack of training or a lack of emphasis. It is not enough to simply put budget requirements into a UFDD and let the franchisees go off to the races. The franchisor should provide a rational level of marketing support and a plan to execute and customize the marketing strategy for each franchise location.

When preparing a franchisee's road map of marketing options, all the marketing materials and methods that a franchisee pays for should be in the plan. The plan should also describe items at the corporate level, such as the company's PR firm. PR is a key component of franchise advertising, both for the franchisor who is selling businesses and the franchisee who is driving traffic to their locations.

The franchisee may contribute to PR in a local program, depending on what you have worked out with your PR firm and your franchise's specific market focus. Most of the time a monthly subscription or contract made with a PR firm is negotiated through corporate. This keeps the messaging consistent. Franchisees are then allowed to have unit-level subscriptions to some level of PR agency support.

Traditional "brick and mortar" PR should be compiled with digital PR to push the noise into the less expensive digital system. Leveraging the positive noise from PR activity and channeling it into routine digital marketing in a disciplined way while religiously keeping to your budget is crucial for a new franchise location.

The marketing budget in a unit-level plan should include everything from brochure purchases and guerilla marketing materials (door hangers, business cards, mailers) to a professional digital store-opening package that customizes social media across multiple platforms, such as Facebook, Twitter, and Instagram—whatever social media is appropriate for that location or customer demographic.

Having your digital marketing team prepackage the user rights, methods, and media being used by each location into an easy-to-follow package is essential to most models. It organizes marketing efforts instantly. The package can be prepared by your digital marketing vendors or internally if you have a seasoned marketing professional on staff.

In store models, such as restaurants or other retail, my consultancy has store advertising prepared for a soft opening when the store is first open for business. This flows into a larger grand opening package for when key influencers (the mayor, school officials, important retail partners, customers) are invited in for a formal launch.

Grand opening packages—including local print advertising that may not be used regularly and radio or podcast ads—can cost a substantial amount of money and must be meticulously planned with the new franchisee for their individual area. An opening celebration for a service business or a mobile model will take a very different form, possibly using an aggressive giveaway or event plan to make people aware of the service. Every model demands a different marketing mix.

There are literally hundreds of interesting marketing tactics that can be practiced at the unit level. With health and fitness businesses, I really like using event planning to pull in a crowd of prospects. They can enjoy healthy food, a professional workout, or a free health checkup to introduce the service and brand. This book is meant to encourage the *opposite* of "templating" when it comes to marketing programs. Your PR, digital, and traditional advertising methods must be customized for your model, and further customized for the region you are locating in.

In addition, when our marketing department builds unit-level marketing plans for franchisees, we like to use a three-tiered budgeting system for various levels of spending, from aggressive to modest. The aggressive tier includes more local events, trade shows, and giveaways, adding more to the cost. It aims to drive much more traffic earlier. A low-tier plan is for a franchisee who needs to do more aggressive guerilla marketing with more modest funds.

There is more than one way to build a customer base at the unit level. Creating a plan that is both consistent in its approach and customizable for the location will reap big rewards for the franchisee and the franchisor.

It is important to play out each marketing method to give it time to work or fail. Many new franchisees give up too soon on advertising methods that require multiple segments before they can be measured.

Measure each marketing method after giving it time to gel. Use the rule of large numbers. Data measured over a longer period is more data. It gives a better handle on the true ROI. The keys are to make a rational budget that you can really adhere to and to customize your plan using the best intelligence, vendors, and executable methods. Then stick to it for the duration of the planned timelines.

Once your consulting firm or marketing magicians finish the unit-level plan and edit the contents carefully, you will be choosing PR firms, digital vendors, and other experts to execute various portions of the plan with you and/or your marketing team. Take the time to create relationships with a wide variety of digital and old-school advertising vendors. Fill your arsenal with the best local tools available.

It is important that your marketing director or team is on top of all the new methods that can potentially increase a franchisee's ROI. Do not get into the rut of focusing only on marketing firms and media companies that specialize in franchise marketing. Franchise marketing and unit-level marketing are still creative processes if done correctly. If you lock in to just one firm on a creative level, you may rob yourself of a ton of unique talent that is worth exploring.

The creative process in advertising is very different from the other expertise evaluated in this book. Do not get pressured at a franchise trade show to jump at the first brilliant-looking franchise marketing company. You may be getting *Arrested Development* when you really need *Mad Men*.

## Supporting the Unit-Level Plan

When discussing the strategic plan for your franchise operation, I went over the first positions you need to add to the company payroll. These are determined by your existing talent pool and your personal abilities in the way of sales, communications, support, and operations.

What I have found out over the years is that a key position that is likely to be added early is the franchise marketing director. When a franchise support office is new, this position generally plays a dual role. The franchise marketing director at this stage is marketing support for both the franchisor, generating the best franchise leads according to the franchise marketing plan, and the franchisee, supporting execution at the unit level.

How much energy is put into each category is very subjective and month to month. The franchise marketing director will probably spend at least 30 percent of their time supporting the franchisees, assisting them with methods, vendors, analyses, and print materials. Unit-level marketing largely consists of methods that are specific to the franchisee's location and their knowledge of local options. Your marketing talent should track the performance of all methodologies that wind up in their budget.

Finally, a concise spreadsheet report of all franchisee marketing methods, costs, and ROI should be compiled quarterly and annually for review by the franchisor. This intelligence should be shared with the entire chain to improve unit performance. Systems for spending should be as automated as possible, with everything being charted at each location through the applicable franchise management software.

You will likely never get 100 percent accuracy on your ad spending, but doing the best job of charting the ebb and flow of marketing performance is crucial to improvement. Marketing dollars are already part of your franchisees' reporting requirements. Making it automated and simple is key.

# CHAPTER 11

# THE FRANCHISE MARKETING PLAN—LEAD GENERATION

The purpose of the franchise marketing plan is to obtain leads to sell franchises. It all starts with a qualified prospect.

Depending on the quality and expense of each marketing method, you may only get one sale out of a hundred franchise leads. As awful as that sounds, when handed over to a skilled sales professional, it can result in one or two sales every month as the sales cycles are worked through. Scale in another sales professional as revenue grows, and you can increase your sales and royalty income exponentially.

Executing the franchise marketing plan is the largest nonpayroll investment of the franchisor organization. The goal is to give quality leads to the salespeople that will add financial capability and build the franchise family. The marketing and sales functions of a franchisor company have done their job when quality candidates arrive at a discovery day shortly after completing the franchise application form. This means the candidates are going through the process to discover the viability of buying one or more units from you.

**Public Relations**

As mentioned in the unit-level plan, a highly skilled public relations (PR) company needs to be engaged by the franchisor—preferably in the early stages of marketing, if your budget calls for it. You can build the perfect model, back it with the perfect story, and put the perfect digital plan in place, but without ground-level noise being driven into the system, the entire process will be much slower.

This may be just fine for some franchisors who want to ease into their marketing budgets more slowly. When you consider how many leads need to be filtered to get to qualified franchisee prospects, making a good deal with a professional franchise PR firm becomes very practical.

Due to the high cost of PR, our firm has flat-rate pricing for various programs built into our vendor agreements to allow for topflight teams at very competitive rates. This allows our clients to maintain sanity in their marketing budgets and stay on plan. There is no reason you cannot make a long-term arrangement like this with a firm looking for loyal clients, especially if they benefit from the "chain reaction" of also serving your franchisees.

## Zoom Presentations

There are a variety of services, such as Citrix, GoTo Meeting, and Zoom, that provide webinar platforms acceptable for presentations. The keys to presentation software are that it is easy to use and can accommodate a reasonable group size conducive to your salesperson's needs.

The marketing team should make up a complete presentation for the salespeople to use for remote meetings and in-person meetings held at events, trade shows, and conferences. The visuals must describe the business opportunity and include items from the franchise brochure, and checklists of how to go through your process, along with other important details about your model.

If the individual company or group has not been given the UFDD, anything that would suggest some earnings claim or dollar forecast must be eliminated from the presentation. Preparing two presentations, one clean version and one disclosed version, is a safe approach. Or just use the clean version to avoid any potential risk.

## Franchise Brochure

There are nine different states (California, Connecticut, Maryland, Minnesota, New York, North Dakota, Rhode Island, South Carolina, and Washington) that require review of your franchise handout or brochure prior to you using the documents for selling the franchise. This must be taken into consideration when adding copy to the brochure layout. Your compliance team must send the brochure(s) for review any time there is a material change to the copy.

A brochure is still a useful tool in both digital and print form. A salesperson may use it automatically to safely describe the concept in writing, and attach it to early correspondence and emails. It is in no way a substitute for the UFDD and should refer to the UFDD when you discuss subjects not for public consumption.

Franchise Science did some homework recently on the formatting of franchise brochures, to find the most effective format to use for our models. We were surprised to find that consumers of the brochures preferred a long format with very detailed descriptions as opposed to a teaser format intended just to measure interest and create a conversation.

Due to the extremely short attention span of people today, I was very surprised when my marketing director told me of this finding. They also had articles pointing to the same conclusion. Not every concept needs a huge brochure, but many of the prospects will like a multipage, detailed format.

## Franchise Portals

Franchise portals are still a staple of franchisor advertising despite their leads being much more difficult to work and close. They generate a high volume of low-quality hits. Leads obtained from higher-performing portals are extremely expensive on average and can be quite cost prohibitive when compared to other ways to drive prospects to your site(s). Companies such as Franchise Gator, Franchise Help, and a host of others are adding new intelligence to their search efforts of late that should push up quality and effectiveness.

Portals have been a staple of franchise lead generation since the internet was just a puppy. Any time a franchisor is getting ready to choose a portal, an analysis should be done by a qualified marketing professional to measure the newest methods, programs, and results. A test period of at least thirty days should ensue prior to any long-term commitment.

Once again, there have been many changes in intelligence-seeking methods, and the results are happening in real time in this category. A "show me" attitude must be present if you are going to take your marketing dollars away from other options with a clearer path. Historically, being on key portals has both increased sales and improved search effectiveness, even if the portal you are paying for is proportionately expensive compared to other methods.

## Join the International Franchise Association

At most franchise events, the International Franchise Association (IFA) has a huge presence, especially in the United States. Members get to participate in continuing education, trade shows, classes, and lobbying for franchisor and franchisee rights in Washington, DC.

IFA sites and publications keeps a finger on the pulse of the industry. The annual and biannual fees for joining are quite reasonable. This is a staple for your franchise intelligence and marketing efforts, whether you are a concept that attends a lot of trade shows or just benefits from membership and education.

## Directory Listings

The IFA has a *Franchise Opportunity Guide* included with your membership that your franchise needs to be listed in.

There is also a *Franchise Handbook* online listing you can join. Do a search of listings when you start your marketing program, and test the frequency of hits to see where you need to be beyond these industry fixtures.

## Digital Marketing and Social Media: The Fundamentals

Building out a franchise website and social media structure is now a foundational add to the overall marketing structure. Many decisions need to be examined, such as whether to separate the franchise website presence from the corporate site or combine the two.

For search engine optimization purposes, putting everything together and having the franchise business page on the corporate site is usually preferred. But the rules of search engine optimization change so frequently, this always needs to be remeasured and reexamined. Some models separate everything out. The most difficult decision of all will be who to trust to design your franchise website, and advise you on your social media presence.

Your social media structure is as critical today as websites alone were a decade ago. Do you outsource your social media messaging? Do you chatter on Twitter when you are a franchisor or just post things on occasion?

## The Franchise Website and Social Media Postings

The rules of the road on websites, social media, and digital PR are evolving faster than many of us can keep up with. My consulting firm has extensive marketing talent that prepares the franchise plans for our clients and the underlying execution strategy of each method. It is available to advise our clients' marketing directors or hired talent.

When we do our three-day franchise boot camps in Los Angeles or Santa Barbara, we generally invite top industry professionals who focus on various aspects of branding and marketing that we do not do ourselves in-house. These speakers make the events more interesting and help us to step outside of our shell to learn new media methods and technologies.

There is simply no way that I can stay as current as the most sophisticated marketing and brand-development agencies in the world on a month-to-month basis, even though I have my own CMO, creatives, and intel in-house. The digital universe moves too fast. My job is to have the best vendors in class to help our clients and us evolve into the digital future.

In that light, should franchisors outsource their social media to save time? Usually, the answer is no—as long as you have your own marketing talent or have taken the time to plug in to the various media all the way yourself.

Research has shown that even though there are many firms who will do postings for you, it is ideal to have someone posting from inside the company, since they would be more connected to your franchise universe. This is almost counterintuitive, as we live in a world where we outsource nearly everything. In fact, I was able to save an hour and a half every morning by outsourcing my gym workout to a neighbor kid, and I'm feeling really good about that (total win-win). But when it comes to messaging on social media, something gets lost in the conversation when the conversation is not from a first-party participant in the franchise brand. Although there are multiple companies that will handle your LinkedIn, Instagram, and Facebook messaging for you, ideally you should be the author. Contour your postings and schedule them with great care.

A franchisor generally is not encouraged to have a constant flow of Twitter conversations. However, having a few well-placed postings of events and articles is fantastic and should be done across all social media channels. So long as the content is created or derived by the franchisor, having an automated service coordinate and post your media and even edit it is just fine.

The ultimate leverage is having amazing PR opportunities that really pop, which you can multipurpose across all your social channels. We have a client whose model is a fifteen-thousand-square-foot dog hotel. Can you imagine the volume of amazing puppy pics we post daily? It brings in customers to the point that the company cannot book any more rooms. Occasionally it also brings in an amazing franchisee lead with complete buy-in who is financially qualified to purchase a large-format pet franchise and happens to be looking for a business opportunity.

You need to create your own luck by having all the franchise marketing cylinders firing on your engine. Hire the magic of well-executed PR. Put social media in the hands of an employee who can manage your content. Use digital vendors. Those efficiencies are vital to your lead generation. What you decide to do in-house will be determined by time versus money along with the talent you possess in this category.

## Pay Per Click

In the old days of the internet, I was taught that the pay-per-click (PPC) option should be utilized in the early stage of a franchise's growth until natural search engine optimization took off. Then the PPC could be tapered back. This may still be textbook for some people; it all depends on the cost and rate of return.

As an example, I am in a business where there are very few full-service franchise consultancies that both deliver and coach all franchise development phases point to point. Therefore, I am not competing with nine hundred places when I buy PPC services from Google or Facebook. As a new franchisor in a specific business category, you must look at your particular performance metrics and do some testing before you commit to a huge click budget.

Across our franchisor base, we have increased PPC activity due to changes in the rules at Google and demand factors at Bing and other smaller engines.

I know this is redundant, but it is *all about* ROI. If you are getting the return desired from PPC, then turn it up for three months. Test it with more dollars and subtract those dollars from an underperforming category. If you are experiencing nothing but noise for your extra dollars, it is time to recalculate and recalibrate your digital ad budget.

## Remarketing

When this search feature first arrived on the scene, I must say it weirded me out a little. I could not understand why every time I went to search for something, there were so many bourbon ads floating across the screen. Launching franchisor ads that chase a potential franchisee has been the subject of some heated debate over the last three years.

On one hand, it seems incredibly annoying for a franchise model to be that aggressive. On the other hand, it works. I mean it is effective if given time to build. The key for each franchisor is to have the discussion with your content manager and digital vendors as to how to position your ad and how to limit the aggression to a tasteful level.

## Show Me a Sign

One of my friends, who is a director of franchising in the dessert industry, called me up at the office a couple years ago and was as mad as a wet hen. He had just sold an area development of six units for Southern California, and instead of being elated, he was breathing fire.

His problem was as follows: the franchisor was new and had just build up a large first-year budget in proportion to their size—about $250,000. They had spent all of it in six months without closing a deal. A three- to six-month sales cycle is certainly not unusual for a new franchisor, but the clock was ticking and my friend was nervous.

Then, as part of his franchise advertising, he put up a simple sign in the sweets shop, saying, "We're Franchising!" A guy familiar with the store walked in, saw the sign, and signed up for six units. It was another two months before any of the other marketing showed results.

The lesson is simple yet important. It takes seven to nine lead-generation systems and/or marketing methods, running simultaneously and consistently, to build your franchise system. Digital marketing is the most fundamental and PR is a close second for most models. What are your seven separate lead systems going to be?

Do not forget a sign on the service truck, a logo on your napkin dispenser, full branding on your food delivery containers, and any other tasteful and clever ways to showcase your brand.

In addition, think about offering your franchisees a reward for referrals. Have their staff hand out ready-made trifold pamphlets so inquiries can be directed to you.

## Natural Referrals and Paid Referrals

We have talked about the most common methods of paid lead generation. The best leads are still and always will be direct referrals from happy franchisees or dedicated customers of your model.

One of the ethical questions I get asked a lot by new franchisors is "What about paid referrals?" Paid referrals certainly do not pack the punch of natural referrals. My consultancy has what I labelled a talent scout program. Professionals from various industries—such as real estate, law, and marketing—who rub elbows with potential franchisees refer them to my franchisor clients. Participating scouts receive a flat marketing fee for passing on information about an interested party, usually when the transaction closes.

If the fee is not tied to the franchise fee in the UFDD in any way, I do not have a problem with paid referrals like this. As with any other paid activity, the fact that a person is being compensated should be disclosed. It is important to note that a paid referral source cannot participate in the sales process. If they do participate in the sales process, then they must be listed in the UFDD as a salesperson. A paid referral source can participate in marketing to the extent of giving you a nice lead, but if they are involved in the sales process without being properly disclosed, you are breaking the rules.

## Franchise Trade Shows and Industry Events

One of the biggest challenges over the last six years has been gauging the ROI of franchise and industry trade shows. A properly executed franchise trade show can be the number-one sales generator for many models in many categories. Even though show volume has gone down over the years, it still brings together a roomful of people who are looking to buy a business.

Remember the constant rule: it is not how much you spend, it is the return on that spending. Would it not be better to throw a ton of money at trade shows and throw out half of the other methods? The answer is a flat *no*. You will go to franchise trade shows where you get more than a hundred leads—and nothing will close. You will go to a small trade show in Texas, and you will get two sales. You just never know. All cylinders must be firing always with your seven to nine lead systems.

What about industry shows? If you are in the auto repair or auto maintenance industry, should you focus on selling franchises at an industry show? There's a simple way to look at this: Are the attendees of the industry show there to buy a business? Probably not. They are there to hear news and look at products or services for their existing businesses. You may need to be there for industry purposes, but you are not going to have franchise buyers walking by every minute.

A franchise show needs to be manned by your top people. Having the franchisor owner(s) there is good, and having your top management and sales team there is important. Anyone remotely involved in your marketing and sales process can help, but the people you want front and center at your table are the relationship builders who sell and market the franchise.

Scheduling for the show should place at least two people manning the table and a senior decision maker (such as yourself) seated in the background to give tablet presentations or have meaningful conversations with prospects. This will lead to future productive dialogue.

Prepared presentations on a large tablet or laptop should be rehearsed and sharp. UFDD disclosure documents should be ready to email or hand to any serious potential buyers when the conversation requires disclosure.

You should not eat food while working the booth, even if your franchise is a food concept serving samples. Professional attire varies by concept. A sharp-looking crew that is awake and rested is very important. The investment is large for trade shows. It can easily exceed ten thousand dollars for a table, and far more for booths larger than ten feet by ten feet.

You are at a franchise trade show for one purpose: to get qualified franchisee leads. Having a preparatory meeting prior to the show is essential. Also plan for quick five-minute talks at the show itself, prior to each day's opening. At the end of the day, take another five minutes to talk about the leads that came in, how the day went, and what things your team needs to improve.

Getting the most out of each show is far more important than the size of the booth. A standard ten-by-ten booth can do the trick when it's tastefully branded and staffed with an alert salesperson at the ready, well-supplied with business cards and marketing materials. Professional rules about conversation, sales presentations, and handoffs must be established and practiced.

At the trade show, you will be besieged by vendors who want to plug their equipment and use your booth as a lead source. Take their cards and wish them a good show. Do not allow them to clog the system. If necessary, take them aside to talk a moment and send them on their way.

When interested people arrive at your booth, have the salespeople hand them off to the decision maker if they are good for a longer conversation. At most shows, there are small, round "high tables" that can be rented in advance. Place one or two such tables at the back of the booth to enable conversation with and personal presentations from the leader.

Remember, you are set up to present. Make sure the serious candidates are handed off quickly to the presenter. You can also offer a coffee meeting or similar external rendezvous at a specified time and place off the show floor.

## Live Seminars

One of the things that absolutely makes me crazy is when a franchisor client goes to a show, spends a fortune on booth space, hotels, and conferences, and then does not find a way to host a seminar while they are there.

It may not be a good idea to have a seminar directly at the show. People are very distracted and busy. You can do it at the show by renting time in one of the venue meeting rooms. Or you can choose to have a seminar a week or two later at a hotel meeting room in the same city. Carefully schedule the small, focused event with parties who have a sincere interest in evaluating your franchise opportunity and are from the area you are marketing to.

Why is this so critical? It is hard to get a confined audience that is walking around in a chasm of noise and sensory overload to sit down and listen to your model. As you filter the people who approach your booth, it is easy to hand them a seminar brochure at the same time that you are handing them your franchise brochure. If you get twenty local participants to commit to attending, and you call each one to confirm their attendance prior to flying back to do the seminar, you will likely wind up with seven to ten genuinely interested attendees to present to. That's not a bad way to leverage a show, increase your ROI, and add these events to your lead-generating engine.

If you have scheduled a New York show and you will not be selling franchises in New York or are not registered legally in New York, then doing a seminar in New York makes little sense. On the other hand, if you commonly do a show in a state that you are legally registered to sell into, then having a local prospect's full attention for your presentation can be very valuable.

Because humans have many different preferences as to how we absorb information, you must cover all bases and be consistent and dedicated in all of your marketing approaches. Do not hesitate to spend another two thousand dollars to host a live seminar event post-show to get in front of a room of serious potential buyers.

There a some very large and successful franchise models that do zero trade shows. You must measure, explore, and define your show strategy for your model. Work with your own data to derive the smartest marketing investment.

## Email Campaigns

Mailchimp, Constant Contact, and many other firms provide the email marketing campaign software your salespeople need to communicate to their base. Also consider purchased or accumulated email lists for large-scale email marketing campaigns. This is a classic example of having all seven to nine cylinders hitting at the same time. Email marketing is very inexpensive and is generally a continuation of your existing digital marketing strategy.

Franchisee target lists can be purchased from multiple categories and sent in large quantity at a low cost and risk. Purchased lists should be a supplementary method of marketing most of the time, as the hit ratios will be lower than all other methods combined. Keep in mind that layering in some low-cost/low-return methods to your more aggressive marketing is good. Cover everything, even low-return strategies, if such a strategy does not require any huge amount of time.

Some of you have franchise models that generate such excellent referral volume and repeat business that advertising is almost an afterthought. For this feat of magic, my hat is off to you!

At the franchisor level, marketing costs go down substantially when territorial referrals and increased inquiries occur, but never to the level where the system is substantially altered and the budget nearly disappears.

Constantly measure the results of your marketing methods while simultaneously giving them a chance to work. Do not downplay the creatives of the world. Constantly explore new and enhanced marketing methods. Once your franchise marketing apparatus is humming in an automated fashion, it is a beautiful thing.

# CHAPTER 12

# THE FRANCHISE SALES PROCESS

⬥◆⬥◆⬥◆⬥

The greatest person that you can hire to sell your first few franchises is probably yourself. As the creator who made it all happen, and the entrepreneur who fulfilled the dream of creating a franchise-able model, your passion showing throughout the sales process is as good as gold.

Whether your personal participation starts at the beginning of the process, when leads are being evaluated, or in the middle of the process, when a discovery day meeting is held at your headquarters, the power of having the owner/creator in the room is *huge*.

### The Qualities to Look for in a Salesperson

The franchise sales process has a long sales cycle. It typically takes three to six months to go through any kind of normal sales process. Many of the leads will be sitting on your call list for years.

Buying a franchise business may be the largest or most important financial decision some of these prospects will ever make. Their motivation levels are all over the place. Every single lead must be tracked, properly serviced, and played all the way out before it is declared a no-sale or put into the drip campaign database. You are not only looking for a way to hire a salesperson who has all the desirable personality traits, but also a person who comes from a mindset or a background where a long sales cycle with a high reward is common.

Examples of this background are former real estate brokers, people involved in business sales or business opportunity sales, or managers from a similar industry who have the will and the stamina to build up a base over the months and years ahead. You absolutely do not want to hire from the instant gratification crowd of annoying, pushy closers.

Although pay plans vary, I advise many of our clients to pay the salesperson a small base, one that is large enough to cover essentials in your geography until sales begin to occur. As a reward for this, I recommend the salesperson make a high commission on each unit sold in proportion to the franchise fee. As an example, one of our restaurant clients with a popular concept pays their salesperson $3,000 per month as a base, charges a $35,000 franchise fee to the franchise buyer, and pays a sales commission of $12,000 for an individual unit and $9,500 per unit for an area development sale.

This is not a best practices or industry standard; this is what was worked out after we pooled the training, support, marketing, and other costs that are paid from the franchise fee. If you wish to pay a more rational base salary, then the commission rate should come down substantially. It is different for different models and is a great argument for not underpricing your franchise fee and going upside down.

Back to personal qualities. It would be super if the person you hire who can work with the long sales cycle also has a great sales record. This probably goes without saying. It is essential for salespeople to have a relationship-building demeanor, not a punchy, do-it-now, slam-dunk approach. Enthusiasm is wonderful, and you can certainly get away with a lot if you have a bunch of it (I hear). But you are looking for a person who is going to water the seeds that will eventually join your franchise family. This is likely not the same person that sells used cars in a high-pressure sales environment.

I do not want to generalize too much here. Some very solid salespeople purposely convert to a longer sales cycle because they prefer to do a slow dance instead of thrashing in the mosh pit. Intent matters. Initial interview questions should hone in on expectations, behavior, sales, and style preferences.

Much like franchisees, prospective salespeople should take a preliminary online test to explore and define the variables that may make them ideal or not ideal for this position. A background check is also essential. Remember, this person is going to be on your UFDD and will be largely responsible for the volume of your empire. "Be careful" does not even begin to describe the caution level merited here.

Does this salesperson have integrity? What associations or groups do they belong to? Are they a joiner or a loner when it comes to engaging with people? What was their method of warming up or identifying with you on the phone and in person?

If you cannot visualize this sales professional as a relationship builder, it is very difficult to predict success with them.

Familiarity with various enterprise software packages and routines is eventually very important. Habits of information logging and following up are far more important to me than software familiarity. You want to know the prospect's work habits to the best of your ability before the hire. When a lead comes into your system, you want it examined, entered, and updated with the most current data. The lead should be called ASAP. Have the potential salesperson explain their follow-up routine, and then explain to them your expectations in your daily routine.

One of the things that I like to do during interviews for just about any franchise position is some form of roleplaying. This is uncomfortable for some people. Push your way through it as best you can. It will likely yield answers to method and style that may not come out during normal testing and interview questions.

When a certain comfort level has been attained, have the sales candidate attend a discovery day or another company event in which your entire team is participating. Have the team interact with the candidate.

See if a franchisee prospect forms an opinion of the candidate. If you are not comfortable having the sales prospect representing you at a discovery day, they are not the right candidate for your team.

## A Typical Sales Routine

A salesperson, whether they work from home or in your physical office, is sitting at a computer. Let's say your marketing system is working nicely. Leads are coming in from your seven to nine marketing methods, and these are automatically uploaded to the database module on the salesperson's screen. You have been marketing slowly for the first ninety days of active sales, and you have about 150 to 200 active leads. These have come in from events, website, social media inquiries, an industry trade show, franchise portal activity, and a few direct referrals.

Your software system handles all aspects of the entire franchise: CRM, finance, royalty payments, support, and compliance. The salesperson—let's call her Jane—is just using the CRM during the sales process now, although she may have to hit a button in the compliance module to send a UFDD disclosure if she is having a productive day.

Jane makes a follow-up call to a prospect from the trade show. The prospect is a man named John. John was given a franchise brochure. This call was scheduled for today to go over the procedures and a checklist for interested prospects. John did not attend a meeting or seminar at the trade show, and the UFDD has not yet been disclosed.

Jane greets John warmly. They chat for a moment about the great time they both had at the trade show. This flows into the purpose of the call, which on Jane's side is to evolve a productive conversation to measure John's interest in becoming a franchisee.

Jane opens a file, one of a group on the right-hand side of her screen. It is the franchisee checklist, and she emails it to John. Once he receives it, John reviews the steps of the sales process and all the steps post-sale. Jane reviews the process with John slowly and carefully, pausing respectfully to answer all of John's questions.

Jane previously gave John a franchise brochure. Today she sends him the UFDD, complete with the contracts the franchisor offers for the various individual and area development agreements. Jane asks John to sign the confirmation form attached to the UFDD and sent it back to her immediately to document John's receipt of the UFDD. Now the fourteen-day clock on the UFDD review period, required by law, can start.

Jane also sends over the franchisee evaluation form (application) to fill out, including a signature block that allows her to commence a full background check through the franchisor's investigations vendor. John discusses the evaluation form with Jane for a few moments to get clarity on all the requirements and why each is necessary. Jane carefully goes through each question. The call ends.

Take a moment to go to appendix E and review all the steps on the sample franchise checklist. The steps leading up to the discovery day will not only yield the qualifications of the potential franchisee but will produce questions and challenges.

Jane pauses to enter everything that just happened into the CRM. Jane does not occupy herself with anything else until 100 percent of the data yielded by the conversation with John has been inputted. Unlike in quick sales processes, every item—even the color and breed of John's dog, Flippy— is recorded in detail in the CRM so that no shred of information is missed when planning for John's discovery day, scheduled for a few weeks from now.

Jane moves on to the next lead, which is a new one produced from the website. This is her first call to the lead. After a polite conversation with Frances, a woman from Maryland, Jane mentions that the franchise concept is not currently registered in the State of Maryland. Jane is not allowed to sell or quote terms, costs, or any other pertinent data with a resident of Maryland until the franchisor is legally registered and selling there. Jane sends Frances an approved brochure and a preapproved no-offer letter that states the franchisor will reach out again once it can legally sell in Maryland. Jane thanks Frances for her time. She then moves on to her other 149 follow-up calls.

There is a company meeting scheduled at four thirty in the conference room of the franchisor's headquarters today. Jane has been getting a lot of inquiries from the East Coast. It has come to her attention that the franchisor did not register or file in all twenty-three registrations and/or filing states, only targeting Midwest and Western states to start. Jane is going to bring in a list of area inquiries so the questions of demand in those areas can be addressed and a possible update to the UFDD and required registrations can be executed posthaste.

***

I believe the most interesting thing about a franchise salesperson's job is the incredible people they get to meet. Discovery days are fun. So are the long talks and late-night dinners where big life decisions happen for potential franchisees.

The day-to-day process of pulling leads, qualifying leads, calling and emailing leads, sending out brochures, sending out UFDDs and applications, plugging prospects into appropriate funders or authorized lenders, dealing with realtors and location options, and putting it all meticulously together in a system perfectly designed for all the above—that is rewarding.

The tools of the trade include a full seminar script in PowerPoint, brochures, current UFDDs, checklists, a calendar of open discovery days, and a massive dataset in the cloud. With a combination of great software and terrific marketing, a solid franchise salesperson may be expected to sell one or two franchises per month. Scaling additional salespeople into your system requires a complete analysis of your program and how many units one person can responsibly sell and handle at a time. Please evaluate this carefully. Measure the workload to set realistic expectations.

## Sales Brokers

Everything has a time and a place as everything evolves. The role of outsourced sales brokers has blown up as more than three thousand franchise brands clamor for leads and sales. Keep in mind that many franchisors do not have the skill sets, staff, or budget to build a franchise sales organization. On the other hand, some franchise sales companies will structure a contract with you whereby a large lump of your franchise fee will be depleted if you use them and pay their generous commissions. They utilize their marketing machine to find new leads and bring you fully vetted, discovery-day-ready candidates.

Brokers are, if nothing else, an additional source of leads for a mature and running franchise. For a new franchise with a low cost of $250,000 or less—as opposed to $500,000 for a typical restaurant model—brokers many times can be the answer to vastly increase lead generation.

Having said that, often I do not recommend a pure broker model as a substitute for a franchisor's in-house sales effort. I prefer that most systems learn to sell their own franchises first prior to engaging with outside sales options.

One of the things I want to mention here is that when I say "broker," I do not mean a sophisticated outsourced sales and marketing operation that literally takes over your entire sales process, your marketing process, and most or all of your up-front fee. Some companies now offer to literally take over all marketing and sales duties for a given brand in return for the bulk of the franchise fees, and in some cases a small royalty split. Historically I have been very suspect of these types of organizations because they can and do cause a monstrous disconnect between franchisor and franchisee. The bonds needed to build a strong franchise can become very weak. Most brands use some type of third-party brokers to bring in vetted leads, but not to the extent of outsourcing the entire sales and lead-generation process.

The broker model I am referring to, which is worth exploring for many franchisors, is an individual, company, or network that provides fully vetted franchisee *candidates*. The in-house sales team then reviews and closes with the selected few. These brokers will also take a huge chunk of your up-front fees, but the ethical ones take no royalty participation. In many situations, such brokers are well worth their price to accelerate franchise sales once the franchisor organization is mature enough to add that lead flow in. The danger is when you hire the wrong broker and wind up with a bunch of cowboys speaking on behalf of your brand in a reckless and careless way. This can reflect poorly on your brand and your franchise efforts.

A typical large franchise sales brokerage may have three different sales reps offering your brand right alongside four sandwich shops, two pizza restaurants, and a rock-climbing gym. This is the challenge with the broker model. If you use a broker as an additional lead generator, you also may overlap on leads you are generating by yourself and at your own expense. Sometimes this simply cannot be avoided; the broker utilizes similar marketing methods and wires get crossed.

You want complete and total focus from your salespeople. You do not want them to spend time on other concepts. You want them to sell a ton of *your franchises*. If they can sell three Subways and a Pizza Hut faster than they can get a new franchisee for your new and largely unknown model, where do you think they are going to put their focus?

## Decisions Decisions Decisions

There are approximately three hundred different types of franchise models that have so far been spotted. There are many considerations and many options as to how to execute each phase of your development, how to operate and train, and how to sell.

This can either be a fun adventure or a horrific nightmare. If you want the former, make sure that when you hire talent, you look for a crew that will be with you for the long haul. Talent and longevity of service are both important. If you carefully plan how you will compensate your team with proper incentives and goals, you can create a long-lasting chain that will stand the test of time—and smile while you are doing it.

## Saying No

Do you and your salespeople have the moxie to say no to a forty-thousand-dollar check?

Let's say you have a financially qualified individual in front of you who is prepared to buy their first franchise unit from you. Sales have been slow this quarter. A lot of things have piled up, but you have no closes. It is such a long game.

You know that the person in front of you is going to be a problem. He or she is a good person but does not fit your system, whether because of a conflict in lifestyle, work habits, or culture.

Are you big enough to stop the process and refuse to cash the check?

# CHAPTER 13

# BUILDING A HAPPY FAMILY

The franchisee relationship is the cornerstone of a successful franchise. How you develop close ties—all of them business and some of them personal—with a chain of participants can be considered both an honor and an art form.

Think about it for a minute. These people, some individuals and some sophisticated planners and developers, dropped what they were doing to invest their time, their energy, and their money in your baby. On top of that, they pay you off the top on every dollar they take into their business. That is some dedicated stock right there. Putting a franchise together with dedicated franchisees is truly an honor. You have their full and undivided attention, and they deserve the best possible support from you in return.

The art form is pulling off the human nature part of the equation. No matter how even-tempered you are, at some juncture you are going to get your wires crossed. You need to have a backup plan to stop yourself from shorting out. Dealing with humans and all their petty arguments, emotional overload, and legitimate complaints can be exhausting if not prepared for.

So who are these franchisee people?

One thing I would teach you up front is that they are *not you*. It always annoys me when people call franchisees "entrepreneurs." They are, that they are taking risk to have their own business. However, they did not create the business or the system. You did. The reason you are the franchisor and not the franchisee is not because you are smarter than they are. It is because you are wired as a creator, and they are hopefully wired as operators. Why is this distinction important?

What do you think an entrepreneur would do if they went into your model? They would want to make changes.

When you look for successful franchisees, you are not looking for another *you*. You are looking for an operations mentality. You are looking for franchisees who want to win by working your system, opening several units over time, and making your system better through authorized channels. You are looking for people who will follow your program. Operationally excellent rule-followers are ideal for this role.

Having someone who improves your system is terrific, and that person should be rewarded generously. A wild enthusiast who walks all over your model, changes the décor, and does things outside the operations manual is not a good candidate.

## Keep Everyone Involved

Many franchisors, such as McDonald's and other large brands, create a franchisee association for discussing improvements to the business and model in a coordinated forum. If handled correctly, this can solve a lot of problems. Importantly, an association can bring even the most difficult franchisee into the spotlight to participate and fuse more solidly into the system. In some cases, franchisees are assigned to audit each other's stores, ride along on each other's mobile routes, or spend a few days in each other's offices to experience the differences.

If the franchisees form their own version of an association, it may wind up acting a lot like a union, although an association is a very different thing. If the franchisor sets up reasonable and just parameters for unit improvement and increased revenue, this is the spirit of a productive group.

Most of our franchisor clients feel the importance of participation most heavily at the annual or biannual meeting with franchisees. This is especially the case during breakout sessions during which franchisees address hot buttons from their bag of issues. Just getting a group of like-minded people together in person can solve a lot of relationship challenges and get various parties back on the right foot.

One of my favorite and least expensive methods of encouraging franchisee involvement is to have them participate in some of our weekly webinar sessions for the models that have weekly meetings and share intelligence and training. Pass the responsibility to knowledgeable franchisees to develop a specific topic for the week's session. Have them lead a ten-minute talk on a question of concern. Ground rules to rein in hard-charging personalities should be in place to avoid monopolization of a topic or turning a learning experience into a whining session.

One of the most challenging things when you have a well-oiled franchise machine is adding products or services to your base model that have not been fully tested in every market. Having a variety of test locations is always nice, along with using online polling or other inexpensive measures to get feedback.

If a franchisee asks to test a new product or service that is not currently in the lineup, they usually must bear the cost of testing and other R&D prior to approval. Procedures for adding new products or services should be embedded in your operations manual if that manual as written by an industry professional. A customizable template should be available to send to any party asking to get a new item approved.

Having said that, there is ultimately no substitute for getting live customer reactions at the unit level. If a franchisee has a suggestion absolutely everyone hates except for them, you have a difficult decision to make. If Ron in Milwaukee wants to add a watermelon-flavored beer to his bar offerings, and previous taste tests have equated the flavor of said beer to vomit, then you may not be able to let Ron test it, even in his own bar. Handle the letdown delicately, as the human who requested the new item felt strongly enough to suggest it openly and must be respected for this effort.

## Creating Evangelists

It helps a lot to think of the Golden Rule when working with franchisees, especially seasoned ones with a lot of experience with you and your brand.

As of this moment, you have not yet franchised your business. Would you say that your existing employees are evangelical in their approach to singing the praises of your brand? If so, how can you create that same enthusiasm among your franchisees?

One great way is to make them a ton of money! Success is always a cornerstone in business relationships. Big success creates big enthusiasm from franchisees. Money still talks. But money is not the only motivation for a franchisee.

Do you get up every morning full of enthusiasm for your business? Do you and your immediate staff have the talent to motivate learners and teach the system that is firmly embedded in your being?

# LET'S DO THIS!

Thank you so much for allowing me into your entrepreneurial thought-space for a few hours to talk about the franchise option for your business model and to encourage you to execute your vision with the best fundamentals.

The franchising decision is a personal choice as much as it is a business decision. It will change your work life completely. Discuss it with those you trust in your business life. Discuss it with your loved ones. Have those discussions prior to making the jump. If you decide to move forward with this journey, take the right talent along with you for the ride. I wish you the best in all of your adventures in scaling your successful business model!

# APPENDIX A

# REGISTRATION FEES AND REQUIREMENTS BY STATE

**Franchise Registration**

| State | Initial Registration Fee | Renewal Fee | Registration or Filing | Type |
|---|---|---|---|---|
| California | $675 | $450 | Registration | Annual |
| Connecticut | 400 | 100 | Filing | Annual |
| Florida | 100 | 100 | Registration | Annual |
| Hawaii | 125 | 125 | Registration | Annual |
| Illinois | 500 | 100 | Registration | Annual |
| Indiana | 500 | 250 | Registration | Annual |
| Kentucky | 0 | 0 | Filing | One-Time |
| Maine | 0 | 0 | Filing | Annual |
| Maryland | 500 | 250 | Registration | Annual |
| Michigan | 250 | 250 | Registration | Annual |
| Minnesota | 400 | 200 | Registration | Annual |
| Nebraska | 100 | 0 | Filing | One-Time |

| | | | | |
|---|---|---|---|---|
| New York | 750 | 150 | Registration | Annual |
| North Carolina | 250 | | Filing | Annual |
| North Dakota | 250 | 100 | Registration | Annual |
| Rhode Island | 600 | 300 | Registration | Annual |
| South Carolina | 100 | | Filing | Biennial |
| South Dakota | 250 | 150 | Registration | Annual |
| Texas | 25 | 0 | Filing | One-Time |
| Utah | 100 | 100 | Filing | Annual |
| Virginia | 500 | 250 | Registration | Annual |
| Washington | 600 | 100 | Registration | Annual |
| Wisconsin | 400 | 400 | Registration | Annual |

# APPENDIX B

# SAMPLE MASTER TABLE OF CONTENTS FOR AN OPERATIONS MANUAL

❖◆◆◆◆❖

## Master Table of Contents

# B

## Establishing Your Business

# C
## *Managing Our Business*

# D

## *Personnel*

## E

## *Daily Operating Procedures*

# F

## Marketing and Advertising

# FRANCHISE SURVEY FORM

\*\*\*\*\*\*\*\*\*\*\*\*\*\*\*\*\*\*\*\*\*\*\*\*\*\*\*\*\*\*\*\*\*\*\*\*\*\*\*\*\*\*\*\*\*\*\*\*\*\*\*\*\*\*\*\*\*\*\*\*\*\*\*\*\*\*\*\*

### Franchise Survey Form

Franchisee: _____

Location: _____

Date: _____ Time: _____ Staff Members on Duty: _____

| Franchisee/Management | Excellent | Satisfactory | Unsatisfactory |
|---|---|---|---|
| Operations manual up to date | | | |
| Licenses and permits current | | | |
| All permits, marketing plan, and pest inspection posted in office or kitchen:<br><br>Occupancy expires:_____<br>Last pest inspection:_____<br>Last health inspection:_____ | | | |
| Pest control visibly effective | | | |
| Food handling certification up to date | | | |
| Royalties and advertising fees paid | | | |
| Franchise reporting requirements up to date | | | |
| Accounting records up to date | | | |
| Unit location sufficiently staffed | | | |
| Customer service standards satisfied | | | |
| Sales levels | | | |
| Inventory control | | | |
| Cash control maintained, including safe properly secured | | | |
| Manager available | | | |

**Comments:**_____

_____

_____

_____

_____

| Franchisee/Management | Excellent | Satisfactory | Unsatisfactory |
|---|---|---|---|
| Phones, fax, and computer systems (POS) fully operational | | | |
| Security systems operational | | | |
| Table layout numbering posted | | | |
| Crew schedules posted for the following week—*shift leaders and managers identified* | | | |
| Crew postings in place (weekly bulletin, handbook postings) | | | |
| Safety and operational postings on community message board | | | |
| Marketing plan posted for employees to review—plan to include all advertisements, specials, and upcoming events that will affect the store | | | |
| All employees in uniform, neat appearance | | | |
| All employees properly trained on the appropriate staff manual, signature page signed, and copy provided | | | |
| Each employee's application is on file | | | |
| Each employee's signed handbook receipt from training manual is in each employee's file | | | |
| Copy of driver's insurance and driver's license on file | | | |
| Copies of in-force insurance policies on file | | | |
| Unit location well maintained and all maintenance issues being addressed | | | |
| All fire suppression equipment inspected and current (not expired) | | | |

**Comments:**_____
_____
_____
_____
_____

| Exterior Appearance | Excellent | Satisfactory | Unsatisfactory |
|---|---|---|---|
| Building exterior in good repair | | | |
| All lighting in good working condition | | | |
| Parking lot, property, and storefront free of trash and debris | | | |
| Garbage dumpster area clean and in sanitary condition | | | |
| Trash receptacles in place and clean | | | |
| Landscaping maintained (if applicable) | | | |
| Signage in compliance and in good repair | | | |
| Windows clean | | | |
| Correction of anything that would detract from anyone coming into the unit location | | | |

| Front-of-House Appearance | Excellent | Satisfactory | Unsatisfactory |
|---|---|---|---|
| Floors and baseboards clean and free of dust | | | |
| Walls and ceilings clean and in good repair | | | |
| Lights in good working condition and at proper levels | | | |
| Countertops wiped clean | | | |
| Windows and windowsills clean | | | |
| Decor clean and appropriate | | | |
| Proper ventilation | | | |
| Comfortable temperature | | | |
| Overall welcome atmosphere | | | |

**Comments:**_____

_____

_____

_____

_____

| Front-of-House Appearance | Excellent | Satisfactory | Unsatisfactory |
|---|---|---|---|
| All employees in uniform with server apron | | | |
| Takeout menus on counter | | | |
| Two- to three-week supply of takeout menus | | | |
| Table menus current and clean (sufficient number of menus for 1 per seat) | | | |
| Soap and paper towel by hand sink | | | |
| Tables and chairs clean and in good condition | | | |
| Nothing on walls without a frame and properly hung | | | |
| Table settings (all in place, clean, and full) | | | |
| Plates and silverware | | | |
| Bus cart equipped and clean | | | |
| Dedicated mop and mop bucket for FOH. Mop is clean and stored to dry | | | |
| Each station organized and fully equipped | | | |
| Approved decor and signage in place | | | |
| Zio Johno's logo mat in place in front of drink dispenser and at front door | | | |
| Approved music playing | | | |
| Each station equipped with clean towels and sanibucket | | | |

**Comments:**_____

_____

_____

_____

_____

| Restroom | Excellent | Satisfactory | Unsatisfactory |
|---|---|---|---|
| Floors and baseboards clean | | | |
| Walls and ceilings clean and in good repair | | | |
| Toilet, counter, and sink clean and sanitized | | | |
| Mirror clean and free of spots | | | |
| Stocked with toilet paper, soap, hand towels | | | |
| Trash bin(s) empty and clean with liner | | | |
| "Wash Hands" sign in place | | | |

**Comments:**_____

_____

_____

_____

_____

| Staff | Excellent | Satisfactory | Unsatisfactory |
|---|---|---|---|
| Proper staffing levels | | | |
| Clean and in uniform | | | |
| Read and accepted/signed employee guidelines on file—guidelines are practiced | | | |

**Comments:**_____

_____

_____

_____

_____

| Kitchen Area | Excellent | Satisfactory | Unsatisfactory |
|---|---|---|---|
| General cleanliness | | | |
| All health inspection requirements met or exceeded | | | |
| Serve Safe certification posted<br>Name:_____<br>Expiration Date: _____ | | | |
| All employees wearing relatively clean aprons. Bussers and kitchen crew change aprons to maintain clean appearance | | | |
| All crew member in uniform, with apron and hair covering on person | | | |
| Thermometers in all coolers, all coolers at proper temperature, and cooler temperature log properly maintained | | | |
| Sani-strips at sink, sanitizer buckets at make line | | | |
| Sinks clean | | | |
| Walk-in cooler floor and walls clean—all health codes followed | | | |
| Kitchen floors and walls clean—also behind and under tables and make lines | | | |
| Kitchen ServeSafe certificate posted | | | |
| Proper food handling and sanitation | | | |
| Proper preparation procedures<br>Recipe book on premise | | | |
| Proper food temperatures | | | |

| | | | |
|---|---|---|---|
| Food product presentation: freshness, quality, and appeal | | | |
| All prepped foods properly stored, dated (date written on label), rotated, and restocked | | | |
| Different colored cutting boards for (1) chicken, (2) beef, (3) vegetables, and (4) seafood | | | |
| Paper towels by hand sink | | | |
| Dedicated mop and mop bucket for kitchen. Mop is clean and stored to dry | | | |
| All required inventory present, ordering sheets present | | | |
| All posting from Zio Johno's Franchise X in place | | | |
| Proper ventilation | | | |
| Trash containers emptied and clean | | | |
| Floors clean | | | |
| Kitchen and cooking equipment clean, properly maintained and working properly | | | |
| Food properly rotated | | | |
| Correct portion control | | | |
| Timely preparation of orders | | | |
| Safety precautions maintained | | | |

**Comments:**_____

_____

_____

_____

_____

Page 7

| Personnel | Excellent | Satisfactory | Unsatisfactory |
|---|---|---|---|
| Personal appearance clean and neat | | | |
| Positive attitude, friendly and helpful | | | |
| Knowledgeable about products (suggestive selling) | | | |
| Conscientious, especially in taking of orders and following up with orders placed | | | |
| Efficient, especially in prompt delivery of food and cash register procedures | | | |
| Proper food handling techniques | | | |
| Timely completion of shift duties and side work | | | |
| Teamwork philosophy | | | |
| Dress code complied with | | | |
| Employee schedules properly posted | | | |

**Comments:**_____

_____

_____

_____

_____

| Safety | Excellent | Satisfactory | Unsatisfactory |
|---|---|---|---|
| Safe use of equipment | | | |
| Spills cleaned up immediately | | | |
| Rubber mats on floors to prevent slips | | | |
| Drains kept clear to avoid accidents caused by backup | | | |
| First aid kit stocked and readily accessible | | | |
| Proper lifting techniques in use | | | |
| All employees knowledgeable of location and operation of fire extinguishers | | | |
| Emergency evacuation plan posted | | | |
| Emergency phone numbers posted at every phone | | | |

**Comments:**_____

_____

_____

_____

_____

| Advertising and Promotion | Excellent | Satisfactory | Unsatisfactory |
|---|---|---|---|
| Menus updated and easy to read | | | |
| Specials promoted within the unit location | | | |
| Local advertising being carried out properly | | | |
| Website posting up-to-date and accurate | | | |

**Comments:**_____

_____

_____

_____

_____

| Point of Service/Cash Register System | Excellent | Satisfactory | Unsatisfactory |
|---|---|---|---|
| Sufficient cash bank | | | |
| Clean and operable | | | |
| Proper transaction procedures in use | | | |
| Stocked with tapes and credit card forms | | | |
| Policies posted | | | |
| Money secured according to policy | | | |

**Comments:**_____

_____

_____

_____

_____

**Additional Comments from Field Consultant** (to be attached):

_____     _____

Signature of Field Consultant          Date

**Comments from Franchisee** (to be attached)

_____     _____

Signature of Franchisee                Date

# NOTICE TO CURE (SAMPLE)

—◆◆◆◆◆—

[Date]

Name of Franchisee
Address

RE:  [Franchise—Store No. _____ (the "Store")
     Notice of Material Breach—Violation of Law: _____
     (the "Notice")

Dear _____:

You and Franchisor "X" entered an _____ franchise agreement dated _____ (the "Agreement"), covering your operation of the Store as a _____ franchisee.

You agreed under the Agreement to comply with all local, state and federal laws, statutes, regulations, ordinances, and rules of any applicable governmental entity with respect to the operation, use, repair and possession of the Store and the _____ equipment, specifically including but not limited to, those related to the _____.

Material Breach:

   You have failed to comply with the terms of the Agreement because you

Right to Cure Material Breach:

Under the terms of the Agreement, section _____ of the franchise agreement you have the right to cure certain material breaches if you _____.

NOTICE IS HEREBY GIVEN that after thirty (30) calendar days following service of this notice upon you (the "Notice Period"), _____will charge _____. In order to cure this breach, you must also immediately and continuously take the steps necessary to ensure that no such violations of law occur at the unit location in the future. If you fail to take the necessary steps to ensure against further violations and a similar violation of law occurs at the unit location in the future, we reserve the right to take more formal action, including the possible termination of the Agreement.

The risk of violations can be greatly reduced by your adoption of our policies and practices for your unit location, including but not limited to, making certain that your employees are properly trained in with our operations manual. Proper training of your employees is no guarantee that violation will be avoided, but it does heighten the awareness of your staff and provides them with training they need to be compliant under the franchise agreement.

**Franchisor Action:**

If you do not cure this serious breach of the Agreement within the time allowed:

(i) _____ elects to and does terminate the Agreement, including, but not limited to, your service mark license, your right to use the trade secrets, and your lease of the unit location and equipment, and elects to and declare your lease of the unit location and equipment forfeited, all effective immediately after the end of the Notice Period.

(ii) _____ sets _____, beginning at _____a.m./ p.m. as the time at which a final audit of the inventory will be taken at the unit location. At that time, you shall immediately quit and deliver to _____ possession of the Store, the equipment and the inventory.

By issuing this notice, we are not waiving any of our rights under the Agreement. In addition, we may take the following actions without waiving our right to (i) terminate the Agreement because of your material breach of the Agreement; (ii) declare a forfeiture of the lease of the unit location and equipment; or (iii) take any action to recover possession of the unit location and equipment and the Inventory:

(a) Collecting or accepting the _____ Charge;

(b) Debiting your open account with the _____ Charge;

(c) Continuing to allow you the use of the unit location and equipment, the inventory, the service mark license, the trade secrets, or the _____ System;

(d) Continuing to otherwise transact business with you or on your behalf, including, but not limited to, furnishing you with the various benefits and services provided for in the Agreement, including paying for your inventory purchases.

If you have any questions, or wish to discuss this matter, feel free to call me.

Sincerely,

**Date of Service**

☐ By certified mail, return receipt requested

☐ In person to

_____

                     ☐ Franchisee

Date of postmark    _____

                     ☐ Other Employee

☐ Dropped in safe with a follow-up phone call/text/ email to Franchisee:

    ☐ Yes    ☐ No

If phone call,  ☐ spoke directly to Franchisee

               ☐ left voice message

Time:_____ a.m./p.m.

Date:_____

By:_____

Title: ☐ Market Manager    ☐ FC

cc:   Field Consultant
       Operations Support Administration – (fax:_____)
       Store File

# THE EIGHT STAGES TO FRANCHISEE OWNERSHIP CHECKLIST

| Stage | Description | Time | Approximate Timeline | ITEMS TO BE COMPLETED |
|-------|-------------|------|----------------------|------------------------|
| Stage 1 Prescreening | Introduce yourself to a member of our franchise development team to ensure _____ franchise ownership is right for you and your city. | 15–30 Minute Call | Day 1 | Review follow-up email regarding the concept, read brochure and website, LinkedIn bios, reviews |
| Stage 2 Conversation | Learn about the core business. Discuss concept, system, and owners as well as the franchise model and its benefits to a potential business owner. | 45–60 Minute Call | Day 2 | Prepare a thorough list of questions prior to the call |
| Stage 3 Evaluation Form | Review and discuss your completed evaluation form, along with your goals, professional background, and what type of franchise and associated agreement is appropriate for your goals. | 40-Minute Call | Day 7 | Both parties complete due diligence |
| Stage 4 UFDD Review | Receive, review and discuss _____'s Uniform Franchise Disclosure Document (UFDD). This document explains the roles and responsibilities of a franchisee and the franchisor; it also identifies and eliminates any potential barriers. | 20-Minute Call | Day 10 | Sign UFDD receipt and return immediately to _____ HQ |

| | | | | |
|---|---|---|---|---|
| Stage 5 Loan/ Financing (When Applicable) | Explore and learn about various loan and finance options for individual or area developers. Request lender information and SBA qualification if applicable to your financing goals. | 3–4 hours | Day 11 | Reach out to lenders to get the prequalification process started |
| Stage 6 Discovery Day | Meet the team at a predetermined _____ location where you will meet with various officers of the company. You will go through the customer side of the _____ experience, get a tour of the facility, and of course, try a plethora of _____ Products. The meeting will be used to determine if a franchise agreement is a good fit for both parties. | 60-Minute Call | Day 30 | Schedule to meet the team and location on a busy day, when you can visualize all of the functions and benefits of the business in full swing. |
| Stage 7 Contract and Terms Review | Have a more comprehensive conversation about the scope of development—specifically, where, when, and how many stores are in your success plan—for the purpose of completing the contract. At this point, many new franchisees register their business entities. | 60-Minute Call | Day 35 | Once edited, review terms and schedule, and have your attorney review the entire UFDD and contract |
| Stage 8 Sign Agreement *Close!* | Sign the franchise agreement and submit documents. Pay franchise fee. Welcome to the _____ family! Hit the Go button with your real estate broker or developer and search immediately to acquire the best location(s) possible. | | Day 40 | Sign and return two original copies of the UFDD and contracts to _____ HQ. |

Printed in the United States
by Baker & Taylor Publisher Services